Public Speaking Kaleidoscope

Public Speaking Kaleidoscope

Rakesh Godhwani

Contributed by
Eleri Jones and Mukul Madahar

BEP BUSINESS EXPERT PRESS

First published in 2017 by
Business Expert Press, LLC
222 East 46th Street, New York, NY 10017
www.businessexpertpress.com

ISBN-13: 978-1-63157-649-2 (paperback)
ISBN-13: 978-1-63157-650-8 (e-book)

Business Expert Press Corporate Communication Collection

Collection ISSN: 2156-8162 (print)
Collection ISSN: 2156-8170 (electronic)

Cover and interior design by S4Carlisle Publishing Services
Private Ltd., Chennai, India

First edition: 2017

10 9 8 7 6 5 4 3 2 1

Printed in the United States of America.

Abstract

Public speaking is considered an important leadership skill. This subject has been around for more than 3,000 years and I love reading, writing, and teaching it. This book is an outcome of my doctoral studies. When I started digging into academic theories to find answers to my research question "What makes an impactful speech and why are some speakers more impactful than others?", I was surprised that there is an ocean of literature available on this topic. I was able to find three broad theories that explained this phenomenon from different angles namely, the theory of communication studies, the theory of persuasion studies, and, finally, the theory of charismatic leadership.

This book is designed to help the reader understand the various interconnected components of public speaking when viewed together from these three broad academic lenses. Together, these lenses make a unique kaleidoscope for the reader to answer the question as to why some speeches are more impactful than others. This kaleidoscope includes more than 50 parameters that engage in interplay among themselves to create an impactful communication and serve as a foundation for future academic work on this topic.

This book is intended for a broad audience including students, scholars, researchers, and professors in undergraduate and graduate schools who want to learn the art and skill of public speaking. The book can also help trainers, consultants, and practitioners around the world who are interested in this topic. The objective is to give them a quick view into the ocean of academic literature and spur further research on, and understanding of, this topic.

Keywords

charismatic leadership, communication, impactful presentations, influence, persuasion, public speaking

Contents

Acknowledgments

This book wouldn't have been possible without the strong support and guidance of my PhD supervisors Prof. Eleri Jones and Dr. Mukul Madahar from the Cardiff School of Management. I am also thankful to Dr. John Gunson who introduced me to them.

I am indebted to my alma-mater, Indian Institute of Management Bangalore, its libraries where I spent many hours finding books and journals on this topic, and its benches where I sat looking at the sky thinking how to proceed further. I am thankful to my teachers, colleagues, and students who encouraged me to teach and write on communication subjects.

I would like to thank my parents, my wife, and my children for their unconditional love. They took up all the household chores on themselves and provided a constant supply of tea, hugs and cuddles so that I could focus on my work.

I am grateful to Debbie DuFrene, who edited the manuscript and made it worthy of publishing. I also am thankful to Scott Isenberg and the team from Business Expert Press: Royston La'Porte, Charlene Kronstedt, Sheri Dean, Nancy Burd, Katie Fuller and Chithra Amaravel for their patience and support for this book.

Lastly, I am grateful to the almighty, the king of this world, whose sweet flute kept playing in the background and kept me going.

CHAPTER 1

The Phenomenon—Why Some Speeches Are So Impactful

Introduction

On November 19, 1863, two distinguished men spoke in front of an august audience in Gettysburg, a military cemetery in Adams County, Pennsylvania, the United States of America. The first speaker, Mr. Edward Everett, was a learned gentleman and spoke for over two hours. He was the main speaker for the day. The second gentleman, Mr. Abraham Lincoln, spoke for less than 2 minutes delivering the historic speech known as "The Gettysburg Address." The two men made remarkably different impacts on their audiences, so much so that Mr. Lincoln's speech has become the stuff of legend and is remembered and studied even today although it was not the main speech on that occasion (Jamieson & Campbell, 1982). You can listen to Lincoln's address here: http://www.npr.org/templates/story/story .php?storyId=1512410

It is said that Mr. Lincoln had accepted to be a part of the event a few months previously but had written the speech only a day before the actual event. Many people around the world would certainly recognize a sentence from his speech that goes something like this: ". . . government of the people, by the people and for the people. . . ." I recall studying this speech in my secondary school. *TIME* magazine refers to this speech as one of the top 10 speeches of all time (Top 10 greatest speeches, 2016).

Googling the words "Gettysburg Address" produces more than 2.5 million hits. The text of the speech and its speaker are cited countless times in academic journals, books, and publications focused on communication, rhetoric, and leadership. A historian, Prof. Tim Huebner, explained that this speech shaped the country and its future to a large extent and laid the foundations for abolishing slavery, inspiring the citizens to reflect on the fundamentals of the American Constitution bringing the country out of war, and charting its course toward a better future (Huebner, 2013).

Many scholars have analyzed Lincoln's speech in a variety of ways. Some focus on the choice of words, some on how it was delivered, and some on the way it impacted its audiences. Some argue that given the fact that Mr. Lincoln was the president at that time, his position and power had greater impact on the outcomes compared to Mr. Everett's speech. Some say that the words of the speech were very inspiring and took its listeners suffering from war and misery to a heightened goal of freedom and humanity. The speech is used as an exemplar in various courses of history, political sciences, and communication and is said to have created a positive impact on the world since its delivery in 1863.

Let's take a more recent example from a nonpolitical context. Technology, Entertainment and Design (TED) is a platform that curates some of the best ideas from people around the world. They have thousands of videos of speakers who are experts in their fields. Each video is approximately 5 to 20 minutes long. Ken Robinson is one such speaker on this platform. His talk "Do schools kill creativity" has been viewed more than 43 million times and has more than 4,000 comments from audiences around the world. You can listen to it here: http://www.ted.com/talks /ken_robinson_says_schools_kill_creativity.

Ken Robinson's speech is only one of hundreds on the TED site. But not all of them enjoy the same popularity as his speech. The other speakers are charismatic, distinguished, and accomplished in their respective fields. Yet, they have radically different impact. The same observation can be made concerning managers and leaders in the corporate sector. While some managers/leaders are very articulate and charismatic in their communication, many struggle to communicate their ideas to their customers, seniors, and peers.

October and November 2016 were eventful months in the USA. The entire world witnessed Donald Trump and Hilary Clinton fight each other with words. As a researcher of this subject, I observed that neither of them was debating or communicating effectively. The debates sounded like two children fighting on national television. And despite the fact that Trump's words, actions, and style were nasty, unprofessional, and an example of "bad speech" for academic literature, he won the election and is now the president.

How does one explain the impact of these speeches through the various existing academic theories? Why is Abraham Lincoln's address or Ken Robinson's speech more impactful than others'? How did Donald Trump get away with his horrible words against women? What theories from academic literature explain this phenomenon? Is it the style of delivery that creates the impact, or the words, or a combination of both? Does the audience play a part in the impact as well? And lastly, what do existing academic literature and theories have to say about this phenomenon?

The point of departure for this book was an observation that I, as a researcher of communication studies, made, that the existing academic theories are not able to explain the success of many speeches that are commonly seen and heard today. An example of this phenomenon is the TED talk of Susan Cain (Ken Robinson also). You can access Susan's speech here: https://www.**ted**.com/**talks/susan_cain**_the_power_of_introverts. You will note that Susan follows hardly any persuasive public speaking fundamentals that are documented in the theory of rhetoric. She even discloses that she was morbidly afraid to stand up and speak in front of an audience and took intense training in public speaking to gather the courage to speak that day. While she is speaking, there is no animation on her face, not much vocal variations at all. Yet, her speech has over 30 million viewers and thousands of comments from those who felt that her speech changed their lives. The majority of them were strangers before they viewed her talk. So there is no "credibility" or the "ethos" element working at all. Her book continues to be a best seller today. What does literature have to say to explain the success of her talk? This book will try to respond to this phenomenon.

Another observation that fueled this book was the many leader/managers in the corporate world who struggle to develop their ideas into persuasive messages that inspire action among their teams and stakeholders. Many young managers are not only expected to do their work, but also to recruit younger members from colleges, train them, and lead them successfully. Their organizations expect them to make sound decisions and influence their teams to follow them. This requires the managers to have strong communication and persuasive ability so that they can be effective in their jobs. It is evident that the organizational success depends on these managers' abilities to lead their teams successfully toward a shared goal (Godhwani, 2014).

Strangely, the education systems that most leader/managers come from rarely teach them these vital communication skills. They are taught the hard skill subjects, and communication skills fall into a "soft" category that is not emphasized. The result is that many managers learn how to communicate on the job, which is very unproductive and inefficient. A lot of young managers also have low self-confidence, which is needed in communicating effectively. A handful are good communicators.

Studies show that the ability to communicate and present one's thoughts in front of others is seen as a useful asset for fast-growing organizations. This situation leads to several questions: Why are some managers more articulate than others? How do they communicate and persuade others? What aspects/dimensions of their messages create the desired outcome? Are they born with these skills or can these skills be learned like any other management skill?

Another crucial factor that fueled this book was the sudden explosion of new communication media. Managers in the corporate world now have to communicate using a variety of media, including video conferencing, telepresence, and instant messengers through a variety of devices (e.g., laptops, handhelds, and smartphones). The Internet and social media also play an important role for managers in reaching out and communicating to their stakeholders. Yet another interesting dynamic to this phenomenon is the audience, which is now often overexposed to all kinds of messages and also has a broader worldview. Audiences realize how communication impacts them and can make their own choices of what they like or dislike.

An advantage of the proliferation of new media for this book is the availability of transcripts and videos of many speeches by famous and successful leaders on platforms such as YouTube and Ted.com. These frequently watched speeches illustrate how presentations are done in professional and business contexts. In many cases, there is a mechanism for audiences to share their views on the topic and the speaker. These discussion forums offer a rich source of information and data that bring out some very interesting data points, which will be useful for the discourse in this book.

I hope that this book will help you understand the various interconnected theoretical components of making a speech (or a presentation, which is a very common form of communication in the corporate context). The components of these theories are like small pieces of glass that create a kaleidoscope for you, the reader, to see a beautiful pattern comprised of many components that answer the previous questions. The book also provides a conceptual framework to help you make persuasive speeches and become a charismatic leader.

Why Is It Important to Study This Phenomenon?

In the corporate world, managers spend most of their time in matters that require urgent resolution and, in the process, communicate extensively with stakeholders who are both internal and external to the organization. Every year, the Graduate Management Admission Council publishes a report on the skills recruiters and employers want in MBA students who are about to graduate. Oral and written communication skills appear right at the top. Bloomberg reports a very similar need and pegs communication skills in a quadrant that is called "Most desired and hard to find" in MBA graduates along with critical thinking, strategic leadership and innovation. Communication skills are extremely critical for young managers; these are increasingly becoming a vital skill set at leadership levels as well and are often associated with how leaders "influence" their audiences to get what they want.

A manager has been described in academic literature as one playing 10 different roles at work. Of these, five roles (i.e., liaising, monitoring, acting as a messenger to disseminate information, being the spokesperson, and negotiating) are explicitly communication-oriented roles (Mintzberg, 2009). The other five roles (entrepreneur, resource allocator, disturbance handler, figurehead, and leader), which are execution-oriented roles, still depend significantly on the communication ability of the manager.

A typical day for a manager will consist of a variety of activities such as attending meetings, phone calls, video conferences, writing and responding to emails, creating reports and presentations for both internal and external stakeholders, and persuading them to particular actions. Studies conducted on how senior managers of Fortune 500 companies spend their day at the office confirm that the managers get very little time to themselves and are always interacting with others (Bandiera, Guiso, Prat, & Sadun, 2011). The ability to communicate and persuade is at the heart of all these activities and is seen as a vital skill that differentiates effective and successful managers from the others. Research on speeches by charismatic leaders also affirms the importance of the ability of the leader to use words and messages to change the beliefs of his or her audiences toward a desired outcome (Antonakis, Fenley, & Liechti, 2011).

Communication is a vast topic and dates back to the birth of civilization. The word "communication" is derived from the Latin word "communis," which means to share. The rise of information technology and economic trends in the world has created thousands of projects and created millions of jobs. Between 2005 and 2010, 27.2 million new jobs were created in India alone through various domestic and international companies (Mahambre & Nadkarni, 2011). The majority of these companies have a global workforce from different cultures working in offices in many parts of the world. The managers of these companies are much younger compared to their counterparts in other parts of the world. So they will have to shoulder greater responsibilities at a young age as compared to their older counterparts elsewhere (Knowledge@Wharton, 2012). The human resources departments of these organizations predict that the front-line managers will be expected to do more with less by leading and engaging better with their teams and preparing themselves to take on bigger leadership roles for the future. In such a scenario, effective communication by front-line managers is vital for the success of these organizations (Lucas & Rawlins, 2015).

Before the objectives of the book are laid out, it will be helpful to understand why this topic of communication has not been given the attention it deserves in academia. If one seeks to examine the famous speeches that have been documented and the canons of a persuasive speech, the theory of rhetoric by Aristotle and the Greek civilization comes into the picture. Considering its depth and soundness, it is not surprising that the 2,500-year-old theory still has a practical relevance to the speaking styles of political leaders today.

Though the speeches of kings and political leaders around the world have been studied and analyzed by many researchers, little effort has been dedicated to studying the messages of business practitioners until recently. So it is not surprising that, as yet, there is no clear answer as to the characteristics of a perfect business speech. There has also been little documentation or studies of the speeches of business leaders, as they were considered less important and influential than magistrates and political leaders.

However, the clout and power of the business class has increased significantly. Of 100 large economies in the world today, more than half are corporate entities and their influence in human and social affairs is significant in today's democratic structures of governments.

Lastly, it will also be helpful if the importance and impact of this book are explicitly understood. Given that millions of jobs are being added to the corporate sector in a global world that is shrinking because of technological advances, there will be a need to have strong leaders who will successfully manage companies. It is evident that today's leaders need to have strong articulation and persuasion skills, and this book could be very helpful in providing a theoretical and empirical framework for becoming a persuasive and charismatic leader.

On an academic front, this book can be a foundation for scholars around the world to build upon in order to create a global impact. The framework presented in this book can also be applied in curricula of various business schools, which can then produce managers who have the skills that the recruiting companies desire.

The Purpose of This Book

This book is intended for a broad audience including students, scholars, researchers, and professors in undergraduate and graduate schools as well as entrepreneurs and practicing business executives around the world. The book provides many examples and best practices taken from famous speeches of leaders around the world.

The core purpose of this book is to answer the following questions: What makes a great speech? What does academic literature have to say about elements of a great speech? What theories explain the phenomena of the great speeches that changed the world?

As a communication scholar, I discovered an ocean of amazing literature addressing these questions. This book will serve as a quick guide into the vast academic literature and help readers navigate through this topic. I hope that readers not only learn what it takes to make a great speech and start making great speeches themselves, but also that they will add to the theoretical foundation to help future scholars and readers.

CHAPTER 2

The History of Public Speaking and Its Importance in Leadership

Prince Albert, the Duke of York, made a disastrous speech at Wembley Stadium in 1925, in front of thousands of his subjects from Britain. Prince Albert had a terrible stammering problem and as luck would have it, he was in line to become the King of England because his brother, Prince Edward, who was the rightful heir, decided to marry a commoner and abdicate. This was now a big problem for Prince Albert. Though he had the right qualities to be the King of England, his stammering was a cause of great concern to him and his loyalists. The people look up to a king as a leader, a monarch, a representative of God who would show them the way. Never in the history of England did they have a king who stammered when asked to face an audience. Germany and the rest of the European countries ridiculed him and called him a "reluctant stammering king."

Prince Albert's ascent to the throne also occurred during a time of tremendous change. The world was just witnessing its second major global catastrophe in a war that would put England right in the middle. And it was also the age of technological revolutions. The radio was the new form of mass communication. Now the king was not only supposed to speak in front of an audience and give messages through the print media such as newspapers, he was also expected to speak into a microphone that would take his voice to thousands of listeners around the world. This incident was beautifully captured in a movie entitled *The King's Speech*, which won Colin Firth an Oscar for his brilliant performance as Prince Albert.

The ability of a leader to face an audience and speak prolifically has been considered an important virtue for more than 3,000 years and has been documented extensively. This subject was taught to kings in the Greek civilization in 350 BC. The famous Greek philosophers, especially Aristotle, pioneered the doctrine of rhetoric and persuasion, which we will examine in greater detail in a later chapter.

The Greeks, however, were not the only ones to address the art of persuasive communication. Around the same time in India, Chanakya, the famous philosopher and economist, taught his protégé Chandragupta, the art of conversations as an integral skill needed by a ruler to charm his stakeholders and manage a kingdom. Chandragupta Maurya later became the founder of the Maurya dynasty that formally united north, south, east and west India into one state.

Though the documentation of communication studies from a cross-cultural context is not the core focus of this book, one would imagine that each geographical area would have its own flavor of public speaking skills in spite of the universal nature of this subject. Before we get into the core of the book, it would be helpful to appreciate how the essential art of communication has been shaped over the last 2,700 years.

Evolution of Communication: A Historical Perspective*

Communication is a fundamental social process. It dates back to the dawn of civilization and is defined as an act of transferring information between humans. However, this is not the only definition of communication, and scholars have not been able to converge on a common definition of communication. Even by the 1970s, there were more than 15 definitions of communication in academic literature (Dance, 1970). To understand communication, it is important to understand how it has evolved from the dawn of civilization till now.

The earliest documented evidence of communication was discovered by archaeologists in caves around France and Spain in 1940. It is believed that *Homo sapiens* expressed themselves by making symbols and drawings on the walls of caves where they lived more than 30,000 to

---

*There is a great course on the history of communication science from the University of Amsterdam and is offered freely on Coursera. I encourage everyone to check it out as it goes a lot deeper into the insights of communication sciences from a historical perspective. https://www.coursera.org/learn/communication

40,000 years ago (Greenberg, 1966). These symbols and drawings were the earliest forms of written communication and confirmation that there was a spoken language as well. As civilizations grew and became more advanced, this spoken language morphed into more than 6,000 languages spoken all over the world (McWhorter, 2011). As civilizations progressed, communication as an academic subject evolved as well. There are four notable eras of evolution for communication studies.

The first era was between 400 BC and 50 AD when seminal theories on this subject were propounded and the subject assumed a great deal of importance in society. Then came the dark ages followed by the light of the renaissance in the 15th and 16th centuries, which spawned a new wave of communication because of technological and social developments of that time, such as the printing press. The third era, which shaped this subject, was the Industrial Revolution of the early 19th century when machines increased productivity, the economy boomed, and the concepts of industries, factories, and capitalistic forms of organizations and countries were widely embraced. The world wars produced important milestones for the advancement of communication because much research was undertaken by academicians on utilizing communication to meet the needs of war, such as encouraging/persuading people to enlist to fight for their country. Words such as persuasion and leadership began to appear at this stage and impacted business and communication theories significantly.

Finally, in the final decade of the 20th century, the creation of the Internet brought about a huge transformation in communication. The Internet brought the world closer, and newer forms of communication evolved and continue to evolve.

These four eras are outlined in Figure 2.1 and are explained in greater detail in the sections that follow.

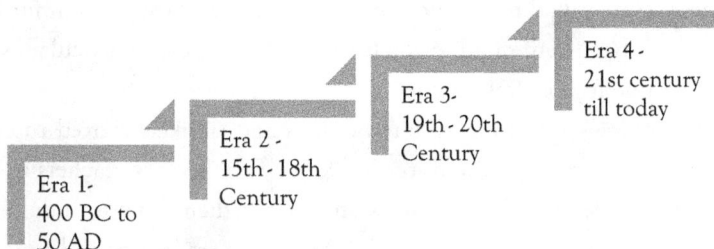

Figure 2.1 The four stages of evolution of communication

Era 1: 400 BC to 50 AD

The earliest mention of communication in India was made in the Vedic ages, approximately 5,000 years ago. It was proclaimed that a good king should have a set of knowledge and skills to run his empire efficiently. One of these skills was referred to as Samvachya or Sanpathya. A model of communication, called "Sadharanikaran," was mentioned in the famous doctrine of aesthetics, drama, and dance entitled *Natyashastra*, written by Bharata Muni somewhere between 200 BC and 100 AD (Yadava, 1987).

The idea of sadharanikaran was to simplify or generalize an idea to create a common or shared state of understanding between two or more people. It helped in defining and explaining how the basics of human communication, through the medium of dance, poetry, and drama, can be applied to broad areas of everyday life. Due to lack of information it is unclear if this model was applied in leadership and professional areas (Adhikary, 2009).

Sanskrit was one of the most widely used languages at the time, though there were many other regional languages as well. Around 350 BC, the Indian grammarian Panini documented a comprehensive system of grammatical rules based on the spoken language, entitled *Ashtadhyayi*. (Kiparsky, 1994). Later, in 300 BC, Chanakya, a famous scholar, advisor to King Chandragupta Maurya and author of *Arthashastra* and Chanakya's Neeti (doctrine or theory), mentioned that one of the important skills that make a good administrator is excellent communication skills (also termed "Vangmi" in that era.) (Latha, 2013). Similarly to today's management gurus, Chanakya emphasized the importance of the competencies of knowledge, skills, and attitude to be able to lead others.

In China, traces of communication studies have been found rooted in the different schools of Chinese philosophy, such as Confucianism. Chinese scholars had to practice an intense written form of communication called "baguwen" or an "eight-legged essay" to clear a particular exam for government jobs. (Swearingen, 2013).

In the Greek civilizations, philosophers and thinkers started to conceptualize an ideal society and its ideal king. They became teachers to the kings and noblemen of those times and taught them how to indulge in well-informed dialogue. Schools and universities were created and a variety of scholars were encouraged to pursue the frontiers of knowledge in health care, science, art, warfare, and politics (Kennedy, 1991). This is where the subject of communication first received prominent mention and focus.

The famous Greek philosophers including Socrates and Plato nurtured the subject of communication and contributed to laying of the foundation for Aristotle to write the doctrine of rhetoric in 343 BC. The benefit of this subject was soon seen by everyone as it helped the kings, nobles, and lawyers win over public opinion in their favor and to their advantage. Public speaking was considered to be an important skill to have and many teachers, called Sophists, started to teach public speaking to those who could afford it. They gave importance to the delivery and style of the message, and not just to content (Gagarin, 2001).

Plato was vehemently opposed to the Sophists' view and believed that the truth should be told as it is (Rogers, 1997). This created a divide among the scholars in those times, which continues until today. Plato's disciple, Aristotle, believed that both ideologies are important and must be used together. He defined rhetoric as the faculty of discovering possible means of persuasion (Rhys, 2004). His work is still regarded as a foundation of communication studies around the world. Aristotle suggested three possible means to persuade: the use of Logos or logic/sound argument supporting the speaker's position, Ethos or credibility of the speaker, and Pathos or the emotion of the audience. Aristotle taught rhetoric and the art of persuasion in his school called the Lyceum, probably the first university of communication studies for future leaders and politicians.

After Aristotle, the subject of persuasion thrived and spread across the Roman civilization as well. Philosophers including Cicero, Aspasia, Pan Chao, and Quintilian advanced the theoretical frameworks and demonstrated that the use of rhetoric could help social issues. Cicero created the five canons of rhetoric, a five-step process to create a persuasive message, which is still used in public speaking and communication courses (Cicero, 1060).

Cicero's first canon of rhetoric is the *Invention* or formation of rational arguments. The second canon is the *Arrangement* of these arguments for the audience. This was a paradigm shift in the subject of communication and persuasion as the role of the audience became an integral part of the process of rhetoric. The third canon of rhetoric is called *Expression*, in which the tone, style, and choice of words are considered according to the audience. The fourth canon is called *Memory*, in which the ability of the speaker to memorize the speech was given importance. This canon is not as popular anymore. The last canon of rhetoric, according to Cicero, is *Delivery* of the message, in which nonverbal behaviors of the speaker, including eye-contact, smile, posture, tone of voice, are given importance. Clergyman Augustine and Laterna and others, started using rhetoric and persuasion in spreading the gospel of Christianity. Unfortunately, this subject lost its importance during the Dark Ages, possibly because of the environment in those times in which the rich and powerful discouraged the spreading of education to the masses (Rogers, 1997).

To summarize, in the era concluding in 50 AD, the subject of persuasion and communication was at its peak. The perceived value of this subject was to enable kings and nobles to shift public opinion by making eloquent speeches in front of other nobles or large gatherings and convince them to agree with their argument.

Era 2: 15th to 18th Century—The Printing Press, Renaissance, and the Rise of the Fourth Estate

The second era of communication began in the 15th century. This yawning gap of more than 1,400 years between the first two eras could be because of the unavailability of much information resulting from lack of innovation in communication. The much needed innovation came from a German inventor, Johannes Gutenberg. He invented the moving type printing technology, which revolutionized the world of communication. Books were now easier, cheaper, and faster to print, and scholars could get access to books, which were previously difficult to get. Authors could write more and carve a niche for themselves among readers in Europe and other modern countries. The Dark Ages came to an end. Education became more widespread in society, and the arts and sciences got a boost, thereby sparking a cultural and knowledge revolution known as the Renaissance.

A significant development of this era, one that is relevant to this study, was the birth of the newspaper and mass media to communicate. Ideas were now being written, printed, and distributed to the people. This was a major shift in communication from the earlier era.

A new element, the medium of communication, was introduced into communication theory. The role of the sender of the message became more complex because now she or he had to understand the medium as well. While the rhetorical tools and canons continued to be used by scholars to create messages, a new theory of mass communication evolved that described the communication process as more complicated. The printing press allowed scholars and politicians to reach out to masses with pamphlets and newspapers and persuade them to rise against the aristocracy.

Scholars such as Niccolo Machiavelli used the subject of communication in political science and its relevance to power struggles. As opposed to the Greek philosophers who opined on creating a perfect society, Machiavelli argued that citizens in a state are constantly engaging with each other to maximize their own power. This engagement creates struggle, conflict, and turmoil; hence the citizens, nobles, and kings must realize the importance of being diplomatic and powerful at the same time. (Belliotti, 2009).

In this new era, the role of the print medium to influence the masses gave birth to the fourth estate, a term attributed by Thomas Carlyle to Edmund Burke somewhere in the 1780s. The role of newspapers, magazines, and journalism had created a fourth pillar of a society: the clergy, kings, and commoners being the first three. (Carlyle, 1993).

In this era, communication was no longer a process of conveying a message from kings to their subjects. It became a process to exchange meaning and derive an understanding from the message that was communicated over a new form of media such as a pamphlet or a newspaper. It also became a means for society to balance power between nobles and commoners. This new idea of mediated communication paved the way to the next era in which communication became a process of exchanging meanings between people.

Era 3: 19th to 20th Century—The Industrial Revolution, Colonialization, World Wars, and Modernization

The third wave in communication came relatively quickly as compared to the time gap between the first two. The primary reason for this was probably the discovery of sea routes around the world thereby shrinking distances and making it possible for people from different cultures to come together.

Other reasons for the quick evolution were the spread of colonialization, integration of the global economy, and the Industrial Revolution. The English language was adopted as the lingua franca for communication between different cultures. The Industrial Revolution created large factories to produce the demands of this new world, and this required skilled workforces. Schools, colleges, and universities were established to fulfill this requirement.

The world wars in the early 20th century fueled a new wave of research, and more academicians got interested in the changing face of communication. The power of mediated communication was heavily used in propaganda to attract youth to join the armed forces and fight for their countries. Persuasion using mass media became an important subject for governments and industries.

There were two significant inventions during this era that shaped communication: the telephone in 1875 and television in the 1930s. These technological revolutions created a completely new and vibrant industry of mass communication by the 1960s. People were able to communicate with each other from their homes or offices despite being thousands of miles away. Political battles were now fought in TV studios, and audience opinion changed overnight if the leaders were not able to successfully debate and prove their suitability for elections. Many academicians from sociology, psychology, behavioral sciences, anthropology, linguistics, management studies, and humanities received grants from universities and private foundations to study the subject. This also explains why communication and rhetoric courses proliferated in universities during this era.

A huge body of literature was developed by academicians including Carl Hovland, Paul Lazarsfeld, Harold Lasswell, Claud Shannon, Herta Herzog, Bernard Berelson, Hazel Gaudet, Roman Jacobson, Theodore Newcomb, Marshal Mcluhan, and many more. Intellectuals of this era contributed to many theories of communication and persuasion studies that we will discuss further in this book. The literature clearly highlighted the importance of communication in a variety of disciplines and the complexity with which it had evolved as compared to the earlier eras. Lastly, it also provided new scientific theories of communication, which helped scholars view the subject from various angles. New methodologies in research were adopted that proved very useful for testing various hypotheses and improving understanding in the subject.

Era 4: 1950 Till Now—The Internet and the Global Village

The fourth era in the evolution of communication studies started with the invention of personal computing devices and wireless communication in the 1980s. This era is also changing very fast due to the various technological advances happening constantly. Today, managers and office workers in the corporate world communicate using email, phone, texting, video conferencing, and a variety of other mechanisms. Another interesting phenomenon that has been introduced recently is social media.

Every day, over 100 billion messages are exchanged through email alone (Radicati, 2013). These messages are sent and received over smartphones, laptops, tablets, and personal computers connected through telecom networks and the World Wide Web. The amount of content created and consumed every second over mobile phones alone is mind boggling.

The political, economic, and environmental scenarios have also changed drastically. New theories of transformational and charismatic leadership have emerged, which have produced a new wave of ideas on this subject. Management education and business schools now look at ways to create leaders who can build bigger corporations, run better governments, and solve social problems on a global scale.

A significant change in this era as compared to the previous ones is the importance assigned to followers and recipients of the message in the process of communication. Scholars began to recognize that message recipients are influenced only if they relate and identify their beliefs with the leader. This follower-centric approach of studying transformational leadership gave a very refreshing perspective to the topic of communication and persuasion as well, which will be discussed in greater detail later in the chapter. Some notable researchers in this area whose works are relevant for this study are Jay Conger, Rabindra Kanungo, Boas Shamir, John Antonakis, Robert House, Robert Cialdini, along with many more.

Table 2.1 summarizes the evolution of communication across the eras spanning the last 3,000 years.

Table 2.1 Evolution of communication over the last 3,000 years

	Era1	Era2	Era3	Era4
Kinds of communication	Interpersonal, public speaking, letter writing	Era1 + newspapers, pamphlets, books	Era1+Era2+ telephone, television, advertising	Era1+Era2+Era3+ email, texting, video, social media
Kinds of media	verbal	print	Analog signal transmission, broadcasting, telegraphs, telephones	Digital, wireless, instant messenger, Internet-based media
Kinds of audiences	Not so learned	Better	Intelligent, well informed, striving to live a better life	Culturally diverse, information driven, highly democratic, and resourceful
Ability to be persuaded	Very easy	Easy	Medium	Difficult
Importance of communication	Low (applicable only to select few)	Low (applicable to larger group)	Medium to high	Very high
Application of the subject	To live a social life, do trade	Means of the nobles to inform the masses	Bring a revolution, express oneself	Everywhere
Sphere of influence for leader	Very small	Small	Medium	Very high
Complexity of medium	Minimal	Low	Medium	Very high

Summary of the Evolution of Communication

Communication and persuasion has evolved over time and is continuing to evolve further. Table 2.1 illustrates some characteristics of this remarkable evolution that are applicable to this study. Communication is no more merely a process of sending information. It has become a process of how people associate themselves with others for a given context and a purpose.

Today, communication is ubiquitous and extremely complicated because of the technological advances and the diversity of audiences.

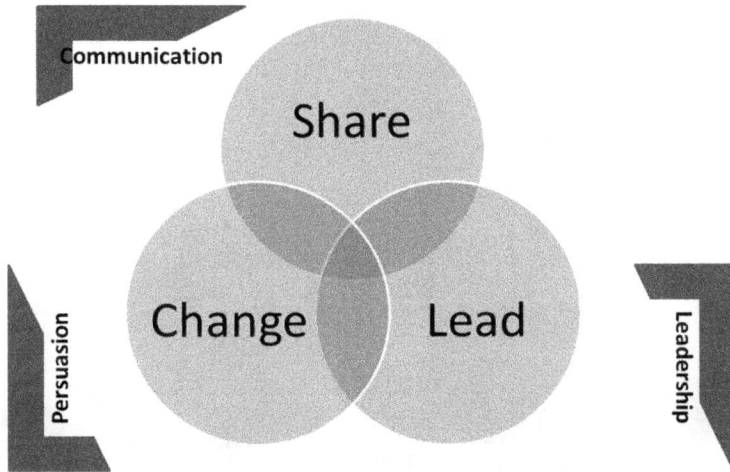

Figure 2.2 The public speaking kaleidoscope: The three lenses

Though the subject has been actively taught over centuries, it is only after the start of the third era of the early 20th century that significant new ideas on this subject emerged.

Scholars started to view this subject from different angles—from disciplines of management, mass communication, behavioral sciences, psychology, and sociology. An important role of businesspeople is to *lead* their teams toward a common goal; thus, communication becomes very important. Leaders must be able to *change* the beliefs of their teams so that they believe in the common goal. The first lens of *change* is taken from the theory of rhetoric for persuasion that was developed 2,500 years ago by Aristotle and is still being used. The second lens of *sharing* is the from the communication theory in management that evolved in the 20th century. And the last lens of *leading* is derived from the modern theory of transformational or charismatic leadership. Figure 2.2 illustrates the interlinking nature of these three forces that shape our understanding of communication.

Communication can best be explained by viewing it from different angles, which form a sort of a kaleidoscope. Using this kaleidoscope, we will attempt to see the variety of bits and pieces of public speaking in an elaborate pattern, which will help us answer the core inquiry of this book from a purely academic standpoint.

CHAPTER 3

The First Lens—
Communication Theory

In this chapter, we will take a look at some of the theories from the first lens of the kaleidoscope, the area of communication studies, that explain why some speeches are more impactful than others. Public speaking is essentially a communication process. So the communication theories will surely shed some light and help to explain why some speeches are more impactful than others.

The word communication is derived from the Latin word "*communis,*" which means *to share.* It is the activity of conveying information through the exchange of thoughts, messages, or information, as by speech, visuals, signals, writing, or behavior. The classic communication theory outlines three critical components of the communication process: a sender, a message, and a recipient. The receiver need not be present or aware of the sender's intent to communicate at the time of communication; thus communication can occur across vast distances in time and space. Communication requires that the communicating parties share an area of communicative commonality. The communication process is complete once the receiver has understood the message of the sender. This philosophy of looking at a communication framework as an essential transmission and reception model comes from researchers who were essentially trying to solve telecommunication problems in the world at that time.

The first major model for communication was introduced by Claude Shannon and Warren Weaver for Bell Laboratories in 1949. The original model was designed to mirror the functioning of radio and telephone technologies. Their initial model consisted of the classic three primary parts mentioned previously: sender, channel, and receiver. The sender was the part of a telephone a person spoke into, the channel was the telephone itself, and the receiver was the part of the phone where one could hear the other person. Shannon and Weaver also recognized that often there is static that interferes with one listening to a telephone conversation, which they deemed noise (Shannon & Weaver, 1994).

Harold Lasswell spent a lot of time analyzing Nazi literature and messages that spread Nazi propaganda in Germany. This was probably the first documented study on persuasive communication after theory of rhetoric from Aristotle. He is well known for his comment on communications that defined the various parts of the communication process: "*Who (says) What (to) Whom (in) What Channel (with) What Effect.*" Unlike Aristotle, whose theory of rhetoric was more speaker centric, Lasswell highlighted the role of the medium and listener in the communication process as well (Lasswell, 1971).

David Berlo expanded on Shannon and Weaver's linear model of communication and created the SMCR Model of Communication (Berlo, 1960). The Sender–Message–Channel–Receiver Model of Communication separated the model into clear parts and has been expanded upon by other scholars. Communication is usually described along a few major dimensions: Message (what type of things are communicated), source/sender/encoder (by whom), form (in which form), channel (through which medium), destination/receiver/target/decoder (to whom), and receiver.

Wilbur Schram indicated that we should also examine the impact that a message has (both desired and undesired) on the target of the message. Between parties, communication includes acts that confer knowledge and experiences, give advice and commands, and ask questions. These acts may take many forms, in one of the various manners of communication. The form depends on the abilities of the group communicating. Together, communication content and form make messages that are sent toward a destination. The target can be oneself, another person or being, another entity (such as a corporation or group of beings) (Schram, 1954).

In light of the limitations of the previously discussed models, Dean Barnlund proposed a transactional model of communication. The basic premise of the transactional model of communication is that individuals

Noise					
Sender	Cues	Meaning	Message	Channel	Receiver

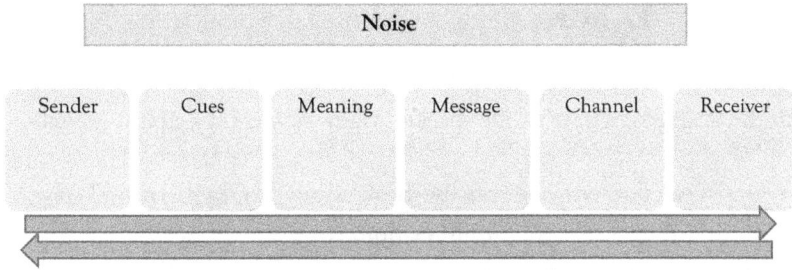

Figure 3.1 Barnlund's model of transactional communication

are simultaneously engaging in the sending and receiving of messages. This process of feedback from the receiver back to the sender is vital for the effectiveness of communication. This model is the closest to the modern communication practices in the business world and established the importance of success of communication and identifying clearly the importance of all four aspects of the model namely, sender, channel, message, and receiver. This model also added new elements to Berlo's SCMR model that explained why certain communications failed (Barnlund, 2008). These new elements were meaning, cues, and noise, as can be seen in Figure 3.1.

If we are to understand how some speeches make impact, we must understand theories that explain qualities of each of these elements and how they make an impact on the overall communication process. We will also look at a few examples of famous speeches to understand how the various theories explain the phenomena of their impact.

Qualities of the Sender

The sender of a message is the source of the entire communication or persuasion process. It is the need of the sender to get something done. In the managerial world, the sender is often the manager and leader. When managers have to get something done, they must have the capabilities to create and deliver a message to the audience for a successful outcome. These qualities range from their ability to speak confidently in front of an audience to their ability to understand and construct a message for an audience.

Delivery Style or Skills of Speaking

In public speaking, the style of delivery of the sender is very important to the overall outcome of the speech. Many factors play a part, namely:

- Vocal variety—this can be broken down into clarity of speech, speed, tone, pitch, pronunciation, etc.
- Posture of the speaker
- Eye contact with the audience
- Facial expressions, gestures, and animation
- Hand and body movements

A very commonly used term to describe the fear of facing audiences is glossophobia. The ability of the speaker to overcome the fear and appear confident is very important to the success of the message. Audience perceptions may vary in regard to the five factors just mentioned. A speaker who is moving all around the stage might be considered too nervous or too confident. A speaker who has no expressions on his face might come across as unfriendly or serious or boring as compared to a speaker who is smiling and conveying many emotions through his face. A speaker who is speaking very rapidly might confuse her audience. The way she stands on the stage can also signal a variety of responses in the audience. Drooping shoulders might signal a lack of confidence, which could lower the impact of the overall speech.

All these factors interplay in a variety of ways, and there is no one perfect recipe. The way the speaker delivers the message has a lot to do with the content as well. The word "*interplay*" is very important for us to understand. And in future sections, we will consider how audience perceptions and abilities are also very critical in this entire scenario.

As you view the video of any speech, try to focus only on the style of the speaker. For this particular chapter, let us analyze the famous "I have a dream" speech by Martin Luther King Jr.. Fortunately, the video of the speech is freely available on YouTube. Take a closer look at the video and try to analyze the vocal variety, posture, eye contact, facial gestures, and hand and body movements of Dr. King. Every time I see the speech, I am impressed that it was delivered so well. King's voice was crystal clear.

He paused at various sentences to give the speech the right impact, raised his voice when he said "I have a dream," and gave it a poetic appeal when he used expressions such as "mountains of Georgia." His confident posture made him look proud and in control. He was dressed professionally, and his face reflected seriousness and confidence. Though he didn't smile at all, the solemn expression was appropriate to the situation and context of the particular topic.

Cognitive Powers of Understanding Audiences and Constructing a Message

While the previous section focused on the skills of delivery, interesting questions are often overlooked about the content: How did Martin Luther King write that speech? What was in his mind and how did he think of those words? Though persuasion theories have answered the questions partly and will be explained in the next chapter, the constructivist theory tries to answer it quite differently. This theory focuses on functional communication competence and the skills needed to be able to create successful communication. Communication competence in a sender is defined as the ability to interpret a given situation, create a message in a particular language, and understand the nuances of behavior and social norms relevant for that situation (Clark & Delia, 1979).

The theory of constructivism was propounded by Jesse Delia in the 1970s and has its foundations in works of psychologists and philosophers such as Jean Piaget and George Mead who thought of communication as a cognitive process where the sender assimilates the perspective of others in the communication. In this process of "social perception," the sender notices, identifies, and interprets things in the world.

A skilled sender will have a highly developed sense for identifying emotional states in others, identifying the causes of their behavior, determining the meaning of nonverbal behaviors, forming an impression about others, and combining all of this to prepare a message. It has been described as "putting oneself in the other person's shoes to understand what they are going through." Another term for this quality in a sender is called interpersonal cognitive complexity.

Research done by Burleson and Caplan suggests that the people with high levels of interpersonal cognitive complexity exhibit a better social perception skill, which helps them in meeting their communication objectives (Burleson, 2010). The second quality of a sender, according to constructivist theory, is his ability to produce or create person-centered messages. Research and experience suggest that stronger the connect or empathy with the audience or receiver, the greater the chances of success in situations that require a more personalized communication.

If we go back to the text of Martin Luther King's speech, you will now be able to apply this empathy theory. The words of the speech resonate not only with an audience who was suffering from the oppression of racism, but also with those from a variety of other backgrounds. Consider this sentence from the speech:

> But one hundred years later, the Negro still is not free. One hundred years later, the life of the Negro is still sadly crippled by the manacles of segregation and the chains of discrimination. One hundred years later, the Negro lives on a lonely island of poverty in the midst of a vast ocean of material prosperity. One hundred years later, the Negro is still languished in the corners of American society and finds himself in exile in his own land.

The words are extremely person-centric. They capture the pain of Black Americans of that era. His words captured their deepest anguish, which he, himself, had also suffered. Thus, his perception of the situation was understandably very high. Furthermore, his training as a pastor and his involvement with people would have given him very high interpersonal cognitive capability to communicate the situation effectively in his speech.

It has also been established that speakers who are able to produce a higher person-centered message have greater social acceptance than those who produce lower person-centered messages. King's speech is a case in point. Scholars are increasingly interested in what happens in the cognitive processes of a sender to be able to generate a high person-centered message. Though the answers are not fully understood, it is believed that the secret lies in how their procedural memory system responds to the given situation and the goal of the communication. Researcher John Greene's Action Assembly Theory (AAT) highlights the processes and structures that are activated in the mind of the sender to produce the message in a particular circumstance. Some of the dimensions that the AAT addresses are speech-onset latency, or the time taken by the speaker to think and say the first few words, pausing, speech rate, hesitations, body movements pertaining to the message, posture while speaking, and social significance of these factors for the audience (Antonakis, Fenley, & Liechti, 2011).

Message

The message is a very important part of the entire communication process. It carries the content of communication shared between the sender and the receiver and is transmitted over a channel. Mass communication theories provide a great deal of insight into what exactly goes into an impactful message. Given the finite focus of this book, we will not address those issues. In the next chapter, however, theories of persuasion will be discussed that will help in understanding our core objective.

Every message has an objective or a goal that helps the sender to fulfill the reason for which she is communicating. In public speaking, the speaker has an objective that she has to fulfill through her speech. If the receiver does not fulfill the goal, the communication process fails. There are two classes of goals namely, primary and secondary, and every communication may have multiple primary and secondary goals.

Primary goals are thought of as ones that bring change and influence on the audience which a sender "pushes" onto them. There is criticism of goal-centered communication from scholars such as Lannamann (Lannamann, 1991) who argue that primary goals don't necessarily reflect a wide approach and focus more on Western and masculine perspectives only. Secondary goals are more "pull" in nature and focus on "shaping" rather than "influencing" audience behaviors. Goals are frequently characterized as being specific, measurable, achievable, realistic, and timely. Overall there is a general opinion that the goal-centered approach does make a meaningful contribution to communication studies.

In studying Martin Luther King's speech, you will find shades of primary and secondary objectives. Here is an example of a primary objective that conveys why the crowd gathered that day and what they were seeking:

> One hundred years later, the Negro is still languished in the corners of American society and finds himself in exile in his own land. And so we've come here today to dramatize a shameful condition.

And a little later he conveys the urgency of this "push" objective and clearly outlines it:

> We have also come to this hallowed spot to remind America of the fierce urgency of now. This is no time to engage in the luxury of cooling off or to take the tranquilizing drug of gradualism. Now is the time to make real the promises of democracy. Now is the time to rise from the dark and desolate valley of segregation to the sunlit path of racial justice. Now is the time to lift our nation from the quicksands of racial injustice to the solid rock of brotherhood. Now is the time to make justice a reality for all of God's children.

Here are some examples of secondary objectives where King is "pulling" or shaping behaviors of the audience to meet the primary objective:

> But there is something that I must say to my people who stand on the warm threshold which leads into the palace of justice: in the process of gaining our rightful place, we must not be guilty of wrongful deeds. Let us not seek to satisfy our thirst for freedom by drinking from the cup of bitterness and hatred. We must forever conduct our struggle on the high plane of dignity and discipline. We must not allow our creative protest to degenerate into physical violence.

In the next chapter, we will analyze in greater detail the theories of persuasion and outline more parameters of impactful messages using a different speech as our example.

Meaning

The success of communication depends on how the receiver interprets and responds to the meaning of the message. Imagine a situation in which a speaker is speaking in English but the audience is not very proficient in the language. This could cause the audience to get no meaning from the message. A second situation can occur when the audience is proficient with the language but did not understand the message because of its complexity. An example of this could be a very capable scientist talking about global warming in English but using scientific language that only scientists can understand. In both cases, communication may fail. This is a very common problem in public speaking. It is important to understand how meaning of the message gets formed between sender and receiver. There are two perspectives: frame of language and frame of talk.

The frame of language considers the linguistics element of the communication process, including phonology or sound system of the language, semantics, or rules of the language, and syntactics or grammar that define how sentences are composed. Pragmatics, which is about how to use language in a given communication context, is also considered. Though there are merits to using this frame for communication, this body of thought is not appropriate for this book because of its focus on business and professional context. Hence, the second frame, which is the frame of talk, is more relevant and appropriate to highlight in this section of meaning in a communication process. In this frame, the focus shifts from the sentence to how the words are said and their underlying meaning as interpreted by the recipient.

The talk frame focuses on the following four dimensions of the meaning. The first one is called speech acts or utterances. The primary objective of an utterance is to convey a meaning for a particular communication objective. This is further broken down in direct and indirect speech acts. In a direct speech act, the intended meaning of the speaker is captured in the contents of the message. But in an indirect speech act, this is not so and the recipient has to infer the meaning from the context. Some scholars also connect this definition of direct versus indirect speech to the cultural backgrounds of audiences. Some scholars have found that certain cultures adopt direct speech acts while others adopt indirect speech acts (Katriel, 1986).

If we go back to King's speech again, you can find numerous instances of direct and indirect speech acts. One instance is the entire paragraph in which King compares how black people are being treated in America to the situation of a bank not honoring its own promissory note.

In a sense we've come to our nation's capital to cash a check. When the architects of our republic wrote the magnificent words of the Constitution and the Declaration of Independence, they were signing a promissory note to which every American was to fall heir. This note was a promise that all men, yes, black men as well as white men, would be guaranteed the unalienable rights of life, liberty, and the pursuit of happiness. It is obvious today that America has defaulted on this promissory note insofar as her citizens of color are concerned. Instead of honoring this sacred obligation, America has given the Negro people a bad check, a check which has come back marked insufficient funds.

The second dimension of the talk frame is identity-work, which helps in defining who people are and how they are taken to be. Two aspects aid in understanding this dimension, with the first one being "forms of address" that the sender and receiver use to address each other. It could be the name (first or last) or a salutation such as Sir, Mrs., etc. The second aspect is called "forms of reference," which can include gender, ethnicity, age, appearance, relationships, and so on (Sacks, 1992). King skillfully uses the words "Negro," "black people," and "white people" to refer to the social classes.

The third and fourth dimensions are called "interactional meaning" and "contexts," respectively. These two are the reason why the frame of talk differs from the frame of language. The sentences, words, and language might have a meaning, but how the meaning is conveyed between the sender and receiver and in what context is what makes the overall process impactful. These contextualization cues can vary from situation to situation and depend heavily on the communication goal as well. They also are dependent on the sender's social perception, views, beliefs, and cultural backgrounds as compared to those of the receiver.

Here is an example from King's speech to explain the two dimensions. The state of Mississippi had a large population of black Americans who had witnessed and suffered oppression at the hands of white Americans, as portrayed in numerous movies, including the Academy Award winning *Mississippi Burning*.

> I have a dream that one day even the state of Mississippi, a state sweltering with the heat of injustice, sweltering with the heat of oppression, will be transformed into an oasis of freedom and justice.

Cues

Besides the verbal aspect of communication, an essential aspect of the communication model is comprised of the nonverbal cues, mannerism, and factors related to the personality of the sender and the receiver. Burgoon defined them as behaviors other than words that form a socially shared coding system (Burgoon, 1993). There are a wide variety of behaviors that impact the communication process besides just the body language of the sender and their recognition and understanding by the receiver.

Some scholars even argue that nonverbal messages are more important than verbal messages. Albert Mehrabian is one such scholar whose work is often quoted in this regard. Mehrabian studied the impact of nonverbal aspects of communication and said that in many cases, the importance of nonverbal to verbal aspects for a receiver can be a ratio of 93 percent to 7 percent (Mehrabian, 2008). A simple frown or a smile on the face of the speaker can convey more meaning to the audience than can his words. Mehrabian's study is particularly useful in interpersonal communication, which is usually one-to-one and different from public speaking, which essentially is one-to-many. But the key message of Mehrabian's study is useful to public speaking as well. What you say is important but how you say it is important, too. In the Greek ages of rhetoric, as we observed earlier, the Sophists gave a lot of importance to how one delivers the message, which was frowned upon by many philosophers such as Plato.

There are a variety of nonverbal cues defined in literature. These cues include kinesics, which refers to all forms of body movements; haptics, which refers to the aspects of touch; proxemics, which captures how space is used between the communicating parties; physical appearance, which defines how one looks and dresses; vocalics, which includes voice, loudness, pitch, accent, rate, pauses, tone, and other voice qualities; and chronemics, which covers duration, punctuality, and the ability to do one thing at a time (monochronism) or multiple things at a time (polychronism). Finally, the role of physical objects in the ambience that could be either fixed or semifixed is also a nonverbal element in communication.

Nonverbal cues have a variety of implications on communication processes. They help to structure and regulate interaction, facilitate the creation of identities and impressions, enable the communication of emotions, and define and manage relationships such as dominance, intimacy, composure and arousal, formality, and social orientation. They are also instrumental in influencing and deceiving others, which we will consider in greater detail in Chapter 4. Manipulation of nonverbal cues can lead to deception, as witnessed in studies conducted on convicts when they lie (Burgoon, et al, 1995).

If we go back to the video of Martin Luther King's speech and view it one more time without the audio, we can observe the variety of nonverbal cues we have just discussed. Notice Dr. King's face, body, and the overall nonverbal expressions. His physical appearance was neat; and despite the heat of that day, he wore a suit to convey a solemn meaning to his audience. His face was serious but not angry. He did not smile throughout the speech. There were moments where he moved his head side-to-side, possibly to convey his disagreement with the situation. He raised his hands a few times to add conviction to his message. He read from his notes and paused many times. All these nonverbal cues, when combined with his verbal message, had a profound impact on his immediate audience as well as on today's viewers.

Noise

Given that the transactional model of communication has its foundations in the theory of transmission and reception of signal communication, an important aspect of the model is the presence of noise in the process. Noise can be understood as anything that impedes or reduces the chances of transmission and reception. In a more simplistic view, noise can be looked at as barriers to communication. There is not much available literature focusing on just the noise element. The reason for this is that noise cannot be present on its own. It actually is a part of all the other elements of the model and is present in every one of them.

Two scholars, Carl Rogers and F.J. Roethlisberger, wrote a pivotal book in 1991, which explained the barriers and gateways of communication from the sender and receiver perspective. According to the authors, the sender can have some noise factors that can impede the process of creating the message, e.g., inability to prepare a message, distraction, lack of knowledge, inability to speak, low vocality, and so on. The receiver may choose not to listen to the message. Even if he does, he might exhibit noise elements such as conflicting beliefs, lack of understanding, inability to process, and many more. The same logic can be extended to the message and the channel as well. The message may have some elements of noise in it, such as codes and meanings that are not known by audience.

The channel may have elements of noise such as poor transmission quality, interference, etc. This is especially obvious in teleconferences, webinars, skype calls, and the recent phenomena of online education. Technological barriers can bring noise in the communication process and greatly impact the outcome. Fortunately, in speeches such as Martin Luther King's, great care was taken by an army of technicians, engineers, and experts to ensure that the microphones, cameras, and equipment for transmission were of the best quality. Any noise in these elements would have been catastrophic for audiences who saw the speech over television that day or on YouTube half a century later.

Channel

The world has rapidly evolved in the last 25 years. With the advancements in technology, computers, and the Internet, the landscape of medium, or channel, is vastly different today. The world is now more closely connected as compared to earlier times, and that reality is very important to understand in this study.

Media studies has been described as the process of looking at media from three perspectives. The first perspective is to study media as objects, and it focuses on the evolution and progress of media. The second perspective focuses on how media is used, and the third perspective looks at the debates and controversies media brings to communications (Peters & Nielsen, 2013).

Some scholars view media as a means to convey a message, while others view media as the message itself. Marshal McLuhan is one of the most active proponents of the latter. He suggested that media themselves, not the content they carry, should be the focus of study. He argues that technologies—from clothing, to the wheel, to the book, and beyond—are the messages themselves, not the content of the medium. His famous quote "the medium is the message" has become a guiding principle for many philosophers and academicians to understand the impact of medium to our societies (Federman, 2004). McLuhan's position can be illustrated by examples of how Facebook and Twitter played an important role in the recent Arab Spring (Rinke & Röder, 2011).

Given the vastness of media studies and its proximity to mass communication studies, this book narrowly focuses only on the media used in business and professional communications—especially presentations made in meeting rooms or over phone or video-conferencing mediums.

Webinars, online education, platforms such as YouTube and TED, podcasts, and the like are the new channels for public speaking. The way audiences consume messages from these new channels is very different from earlier days. This particular element of the communication process is best understood from the theories of mass communication and is beyond the scope of this book. In the example of Martin Luther King's speech, the channel was the microphone and audio speakers, the television, radio, the print medium, and now the Internet.

Receiver/Audience

The entire process of communication hinges not only on the sender, but also on the equal involvement of the recipient. So it is very important to probe this element of Barnlund's model in academic literature further. In Chapter 5, we will again look into this element from the view of followers in leadership studies. Presently, we will take another look at the constructivism theory that explains three fundamental processes for a skillful communicator.

The first two fundamental processes—social perception or interpersonal cognitive complexity and human-centered message creation ability—fit the sender and explain why some senders are more skilled than others. The third process from the theory of constructivism, called message reception ability, explains why some receivers are more skilled than others. Every message reflects a meaning, intention, and a motive of the sender. The way a receiver will understand, interpret, and respond to this message will depend on the ability to go in-depth into the message and process it from all aspects. The ability to process in-depth is influenced by a variety of factors including educational background; relevance and importance of the topic to the recipient's priorities; maturity to understand the message; ability to decode, think, analyze, and make an informed assessment; intelligence and IQ; and audio and listening abilities.

In Chapter 4, we will look at a theory of persuasion that explains what kind of factors impact the audience. This theory, called the elaboration likelihood model (ELM), explains that highly involved and aware audiences will react differently to the message and topic than those who are less involved and aware (Hewes, 1995; O'Keefe, 1990a, 1990b). We can look once again at Martin Luther King's speech for an example of ELM. Audiences who are from a similar cultural background as King, or have experienced a similar fate of that explained by King, are more directly involved and aware audiences as compared to those who have never experienced the described situation. Many of us were born in a more recent era when racial oppression was much less than in the 1960s, so we could also belong to the second category. The ELM model explains that highly aware and involved audiences are impacted more by the content of the speech as compared to the style of the delivery. The model also highlights that less aware and involved audiences are impacted more by the style of the speaker as compared to the content of the speech. It is therefore not surprising that much analyses of Martin Luther King's speech has focused more on his delivery style, his tone, his actions, and his charisma as seen by the audience rather than on his words.

Another example of this ELM phenomena is the reaction of audiences watching the recent Trump–Clinton–Sanders US presidential debates. Clinton falling down and being rushed away or Trump making faces at his opponents had more impact on audiences around the world who were less aware and involved with the election than on the American audience who was more directly aware and involved.

Summary of the Factors That Impact the Communication Process

In summary, Table 3.1 reflects the factors of the communication process as defined in literature. This table includes the more recently described factors, as compared to the simplistic model reflected in Figure 3.1 earlier in the chapter.

These factors engage in interplay among themselves, which explains why some speeches and speakers are better than others. Keeping the audience factors constant, a speaker who has better delivery powers, appears confident, and speaks words that are simple to follow will probably be more impactful than a speaker who does not speak with confidence or uses words that are difficult to understand. Table 3.1 also helps us understand the role of the recipient in this entire process. Keeping other factors constant, if the recipient does not have the maturity to understand the speech or appreciate the speaker, the speech will not be successful. So it is important for the speaker to apply cognitive powers as explained earlier to understand the kind of audience and choose his words and style accordingly. A poor choice of medium or a technical glitch could also cause a message to fail regardless of who the speaker or audience is.

Communication theory gives a good starting point for us to understand the various parameters that engage in interplay among themselves to make a speech successful. But it still does not explain why despite having the best speaker who has chosen the simplest possible words over a clear medium, the audience fails to respond favorably. This is where our second lens of persuasion theory comes in. This lens is explained in the next chapter.

Table 3.1 Factors that impact communication as outline from the lens of communication theory

Sender	Cues	Meaning	Noise	Channel	Message Factors	Recipient
Delivery skills	Kinesics	Speech-act	Sender	Clarity	Person-centered message	Maturity
Social perception	Haptics	Direct or Indirect	Recipient	Ease of use	Verbal or nonverbal	Involvement
Interpersonal cognitive complexity	Proxemics	Identity	Channel		Push or pull (influencing or shaping)	Interpersonal cognitive complexity
Communication competence	Vocalics	Interactional	Message			
Quickness to respond	Chronemics	Context				
Ability to process						
Latency of speech						

CHAPTER 4

The Second Lens— Persuasion

We now move to our second lens of this kaleidoscope: the lens of persuasion. Imagine you are a young manager who works for a company that produces and promotes vegan food. You have been called to give a presentation on the benefits of adopting vegan cuisine to a select audience of a large multinational company. What would you say to them?

I give this assignment to my students in my communication courses. Usually, the speaker gives a lot of logical arguments to prove that vegan cuisine is healthier than the others. Some speakers speak on cruelty to animals and tell their audiences to become vegans and protect animals. Now all these are absolutely correct thoughts and fully supported by the communication theory lens we covered in the earlier chapter. But it amazes me to see that the moment these sentences are spoken, the audience becomes defensive. Many times, I have seen this topic lead to a healthy and sometimes unhealthy debate. So, clearly, the communication theories are not enough for such kind of topics.

Though public speaking is the act of speaking in front of an audience, a critical objective of public speaking in the business world is to get something done. Managers are expected to speak to their clients, superiors, teams, and stakeholders and influence them to do what they want them to do. This is where failure occurs with the lens of communication theory that focuses on sharing. So we need a second lens to view the public speaking phenomenon and understand how to influence a change in audiences. This is where the theories of persuasion are very helpful.

What Is Persuasion

Persuasion is defined as human communication designed to influence others by modifying their beliefs, values, and attitudes (Simons, 1976). From this definition, we understand that persuasion is indeed a communication process. This definition also brings forth a few new terms that need to be fully understood: attitudes, beliefs, and values. Attitudes, beliefs, and values are seen as orientations of mind that influence our behavior. Some researchers claim that the objective of persuasion is to bring about an attitude change that could influence the behavior of the person to whom it is directed (Beisecker & Parson, 1972). Lastly, this definition identifies the following features of persuasive communication: (1) it has a purpose or an objective; (2) it is used to achieve the objective of the persuader; (3) the recipient is free to choose whether to comply with the objective or not; and (4) the entire process depends on the speaker/persuader communicating with the recipient (Simons, 1986). So what factors or parameters contribute to the success of a persuasive message? The literature from the days of Aristotle until today has identified four groups of persuasive factors (O'Keefe, 1990a, 1990b):

- Speaker or source factors
- Message factors
- Receiver and contextual factors
- Attitudes and actions.

The success of the persuasive effort depends on not one or two but an interplay of various aspects of these factors. There are many theories that help us understand the beliefs and attitudes of the audiences for a successful outcome. Some of them that are relevant for this study are explained in the following sections.

Social Judgment Theory

This theory suggests that audiences have their own positions on the topic, which the persuader wants to persuade them on. These views or positions could come from a variety of factors including their upbringing,

educational background, cultural influences, and many more relevant social factors. The attitude change of the recipient on the topic will depend
on his own position and advocacy on the topic. If the recipient's position
on the topic is similar or within a range of acceptable latitude of the message, the chances for success of the message will be higher. However, if the
position of the recipient is considerably different from that of the message, the message has a greater chance of failure (Doherty & Kurz, 1996).

Information Integration Model of Attitude

Social judgment theory explains the concept of the audience's position on
a particular topic and the latitude of acceptance on changing individuals' beliefs. But often the belief held by a recipient on the topic might be
in opposition with the persuader because of various underlying salient
beliefs and their strengths. A more recent theory, called the Summative
Model, explains the phenomenon more completely and puts more emphasis on the recipient's belief system for the persuader to prepare the
message (Fishbein, 1991). Simply put, this theory suggests that the overall position of a recipient on a subject is a summation of the various salient beliefs and the evaluations of those beliefs at that point. So it might
happen that the recipient's position on a topic can change if the persuader
breaks the position into multiple salient positions and drafts the message
accordingly. The summation of these changes can then bring about attitude change. Some scholars have suggested that a newer weighted average
model can be an alternative to a summative model (Anderson, 1965).

Cognitive Dissonance Theory

This theory is quite popular in understanding decision making and is also
used in explaining persuasion. Developed by Leon Festinger in 1957, this
theory explores the relationships of cognitions or thoughts in our minds
and the effects they have on our lives. The central idea of this theory is that
all of us strive to reduce dissonance, or the uncomfortable state of having
inconsistent thoughts. Persuaders adopt different tactics or strategies; and
while they may not be successful in reducing the dissonance, they strive
to make a change in the thoughts of the audience (Harmon-Jones, 2002).

Elaboration Likelihood Model

The Elaboration Likelihood Model, developed by Richard Petty and John Cacioppo, is based on the idea that, depending on how the information is elaborated by the speaker, the receiver will engage and respond differently. The model offers two ways to persuade. The first approach is called the Central Approach in which the speaker elaborates the issue and provides logical arguments that are relevant to the central issue of persuasion. The second approach of changing the audiences is the peripheral approach in which the elaboration is less. The change element could be a simple likability factor of the speaker or any other peripheral cue that can help the audience engage with the speaker better. Another way to understand both the approaches is to think of the Central Approach as a more direct method and the peripheral approach as an indirect method to engage the listeners on the topic and persuade them (Petty, Priester, & Brinol, 2009).

To understand how all these theories work, let us go back to our example we discussed at the beginning of the chapter—a manager has to promote vegan products to an audience. The moment he says that "going vegan reduces cruelty to animals," the audience members who believe that vegetarianism is kinder to animals will support his claim and agree to adopt vegan products. But other audience members who believe that being a nonvegetarian is how they are by birth and by the natural law of the food chain will react in a variety of ways. Some of them might just stop listening. Some might get defensive. Some might even debate. All the four theories that have been mentioned above are at work here. So it is extremely important to understand the audience's beliefs, attitudes, and thoughts from the view of these four theories and then plan the communication.

In an earlier chapter, we discussed how speakers with high interpersonal cognitive abilities understand their audiences better and hence prepare better messages. But that theory did not address how to understand the audience. The above four theories now give some kind of explanation and complete that chain of understanding an audience's beliefs and attitudes to create a persuasive message that changes them.

A great example of a speech that reflects understanding of the beliefs of the audience and applies the theories of persuasion was given by Graham Hill and posted to TED in 2010. The title of the speech is "Weekday Vegetarian." You can view the video at https://www.ted.com /talks/graham_hill_weekday_vegetarian. We will use this speech as an exemplar for this chapter. Here is a comment from his speech that outlines how well he understands the deep beliefs involved in people's (especially nonvegetarians') eating habits:

> So why was I stalling? I realized that what I was being pitched was a binary solution. It was either you're a meat eater or you're a vegetarian, and I guess I just wasn't quite ready. Imagine your last hamburger. So my common sense, my good intentions, were in conflict with my taste buds. And I'd commit to doing it later, and not surprisingly, later never came. Sound familiar?

I have been a nonvegetarian myself and later converted to vegetarianism 5 years ago. I can so relate to Hill's words. Deep inside, I wanted to stop eating meat. But I loved eating a rich chicken butter masala with naans. My cognitive dissonance was so high that instead of changing my behavior, I changed my actions to avoid it. My social judgment on this topic stemmed from my belief that I could get nonvegetarian food anywhere in the world as compared to vegetarian food. I am sure many other readers would relate to Hill's words in their own ways that spring from their own social judgment on this topic.

Source Factors for Persuasion

Considerable research attention has been paid to studying how the characteristics of the speaker influence the outcomes of the persuasive message. The initiation of the persuasion process begins from the source or the speaker. The source factors are also mentioned in the famous theory of rhetoric by Aristotle. In that theory, Aristotle explained the interplay of three factors for persuasion, also known as the rhetoric triangle of Ethos, Pathos, and Logos. Ethos conveys the nature of the source or the communicator of the message, and is the focus of this section. The other two will be covered separately in later sections. There are a variety of characteristics of the source that impact the persuasive outcome.

Credibility of the Source

Credibility is an important characteristic of the source that impacts the persuasion process. It is seen, perceived, or judged by the recipient of the message or the audience. The audience understands and knows that the speaker has a motive, which is in the message. This gives rise to certain expectations, biases, and attitudes toward the speaker in the minds of the members of the audience. There are two broad biases that the audiences have for speakers. The first is the knowledge bias and the second is called the reporting bias. Simply put, the audience wants to know whether the speaker has the knowledge on the topic and whether she has an honest opinion about it. In other words, audiences will be less agreeable to a speaker who they perceive is giving wrong information or is misleading them.

Studies show that there is a correlation between the outcome of the message and the credibility of the source. If audiences react positively to the message and know that the source is highly credible, then a persuasive outcome is more likely. But if the audience doesn't accept the logic of the argument, then high source credibility in itself is not sufficient to bring about a favorable response (Tormala, Brinol, & Petty, 2006). Researchers also found that the effect of communicator's credibility on the audience is dependent on various factors including the involvement of the audience with the topic, the timing of identification of the communicator's credibility (either before or after the message is conveyed), and the attitude of the audience toward the subject (Anderson & Clevenger, 1963; Self, 2014)

The speaker must demonstrate certain dimensions in his credibility to address the biases and make the persuasion process successful:

1. **Expertise** or **competence to overcome knowledge bias**: The competence dimension of the communicator is defined as the ability to demonstrate expertise or authority to speak on the topic. It is also referred to as authoritativeness or qualification (Bromme, Rambow, & Nückles, 2001). The audience assesses how well the source knows the truth of the topic through his experience, knowledge or qualification, and intelligence on the subject. Research on how viewers of news on television make or change opinions show that opinion changes significantly if the person speaking on TV is venerated as an

expert. There is a better chance of people accepting the views of an expert or taking them seriously (Cialdini, 2001).

2. **Trustworthiness to overcome reporting bias**: The trustworthiness dimension is defined by the character or personal integrity of the communicator on the topic. It is also called reliability. The audience assesses whether the speaker is honest about the topic himself, whether he has any hidden agendas and whether he is stating the message fairly without misleading them. Research on political candidates showed that voters supported candidates who had no prior expertise in politics when they felt that the candidate had integrity and was perceived to be sincere and honest (Abramson, et al., 2009).

These two dimensions of credibility are very generic and vary between audiences, circumstances, and the type of message. No two recipients will judge the competence and trustworthiness dimension of the communicator in the same way. They are greatly influenced by a variety of factors that engage in interplay among themselves:

- **Education, Occupation, and Experience**: This factor is important for the Expertise dimension. The audiences will have more confidence in the message if it is coming from a speaker who is an expert on the topic. Educational degrees and background are one of the measures of expertise that the audience relates to. The titles, designation, position of the speaker, and the occupation he belongs to, if relevant to the topic, is also another factor. The number of years of seniority or experience in the industry is an additional factor. In today's highly connected world, it is easy to determine credibility. Online bios and LinkedIn profiles of managers in the corporate sector are readily available. Studies also show that if the speaker mentions the sources of his/her evidence in the message, the audience's perceptions of his/her credibility improve slightly (Reinard, 1988).

- **Fluency in speaking**: Audiences gauge the fluency of delivery and the confidence of the speaker to judge the trustworthiness of the speaker on the topic. Some speakers are very confident and demonstrate that they know the topic well. But researchers found out that despite the speaker being very knowledgeable, minor characteristics in the speaker's oral communications, such as repetition of words, using too many filler words like "uh," etc., or looking tense may cause the audience to become disinterested and unfavorable to the topic (McCroskey & Mehrley, 1969; McCroskey, 2006). Studies have also been done on the speed of speaking and the correlation to the source credibility factors, but these investigations haven't resulted in concrete findings.

- **Personal position on the topic**: The audience's perception of the speaker's trustworthiness varies according to the speaker's personal position on the topic. Studies show that if the speaker has a biased view of the topic, then it confirms with the audience's expectations for the reporting bias, which causes them to trust the speaker less. But if the speaker gives a fair unbiased view or even takes a view totally opposite to what the audience expects from him, the audience reacts favorably to the speaker and the topic (Burgoon & Poire, 1993).

- **Likability of the speaker**: The receiver's liking toward the speaker can influence her judgments and attitudes about trustworthiness. It has been shown repeatedly that a likable person is more successful in persuading his audience. The dimensions of likability are quite varied and range from appearance and gender to behavioral traits including courtesy, friendliness, voice quality, and other visible personality attributes. Another factor that plays a role here is the use of humor in the message unless it is inappropriate for the topic or the audience. The way liking of the communicator impacts the persuasive outcomes on audiences also varies significantly. Research indicates that an audience generally prefers the dimension of credibility in a communicator more than the dimension of liking (Simons, Berkowitz, & Moyer, 1970). Liking and involvement are also correlated. If the audience is closely involved with the topic, then the effect on the persuasive outcome of liking the communicator is minimal. It has also been observed that a disliked communicator can have a greater persuasive impact on the audience if his credibility is very high among audiences. (Zimbardo, et al., 1965). Acknowledgement of the audience by a speaker, including taking someone's name or thanking the audience for their time have also been observed as ways to increase likability (Seiter & Weger, 2010).

- **Similarity or Kinship**: This factor becomes influential when receivers perceive similarities between themselves and the speaker, such as speaking the same language, being alumni of the same college, having the same first or last name, and many more such characteristics. The relationship is quite complex, and there could be infinite possible similarities, including age, occupation, attitudes, physique, income, gender, education, speech dialect, personality, ethnicity, political affiliation, interpersonal style, clothing preferences, etc. Researchers believe that these factors are more significant when the speaker is making a personal and emotional appeal to the audience. (Brock, 1965). Logically, a greater similarity between the communicator and the audience would have a greater influence on the persuasive outcome; hence, it is important for communicators to emphasize the commonalities between themselves and their audiences. However, in certain circumstances, similarities have been found to enhance persuasive effectiveness but also inhibit them in other circumstances. (Goethals & Nelson, 1973; Mills & Kimble, 1973).

- **Physical appearance**: Many studies show that the physical attractiveness of a speaker has an influence on the recipient's perception of the trustworthiness of the speaker. Reasons for this could be that audiences pay more attention to a speaker who looks and dresses better, and a positive appearance increases likability. There are cultural aspects as well. Some cultures may find wearing casual clothes in the workplace acceptable; others may not. Under these conditions, a speaker who is inappropriately dressed for a certain culture may not be liked by the audiences, which will have an indirect impact on the overall outcome. It has also been observed, however, that physically attractive communicators are not always successful in getting a persuasive outcome for a variety of reasons (Maddux & Rogers, 1980). And in some cases, it was found that physical attractiveness had less or no effect on their audiences as compared to unattractive counterparts (Cooper, Darley, & Henderson, 1974). Although there has been a mixed view on this factor, a general consensus is that physical attractiveness plays an indirect role in the audience's liking the communicator.

In summary, the factors of the communicator that are most likely to affect the persuasive outcome are credibility and liking. All other characteristics of the communicator, including similarity with the audience and physical attractiveness, indirectly influence the first two factors and play a role in influencing the outcomes of persuasiveness on the audience.

Going back to Graham Hill's TED talk, let us see if these factors we have been discussing were visible in his speech. In the beginning of this speech, he spelled out his own position on the topic very openly, discussed his family background and a past rooted in a philosophy of being nature-friendly, and also attempted to minimize the reporting biases of the audience.

About a year ago, I asked myself a question: "Knowing what I know, why am I not a vegetarian?" After all, I'm one of the green guys: I grew up with hippie parents in a log cabin. I started a site called TreeHugger—I care about this stuff.

His appearance was simple, neat, and appropriate for the occasion. He brought out similarities and kinship factors with the audience, such as in this sentence:

I also knew that I'm not alone. We as a society are eating twice as much meat as we did in the 50s. So what was once the special little side treat now is the main, much more regular.

He gave good examples and data, which made his expertise on the topic stand out with the audience and reduce the knowledge biases. Here are some examples:

I knew that eating a mere hamburger a day can increase my risk of dying by a third. Cruelty: I knew that the 10 billion animals we raise each year for meat are raised in factory farm conditions that we, hypocritically, wouldn't even consider for our own cats, dogs and other pets. Environmentally, meat, amazingly, causes more emissions than all of transportation combined: cars, trains, planes, buses, boats, all of it. And beef production uses 100 times the water that most vegetables do.

In summary, Graham Hill effectively biases the audience by skillfully using a variety of techniques to win them over.

Message Factors for Persuasion

As explained previously, there are many theories that help explain how the beliefs and attitudes held by audiences impact the persuasive outcome, namely the social judgment theory, information integration theory, cognitive dissonance theory, and elaboration likelihood theory. In this section, studies on the effects of the factors of a message on persuasion are reviewed. The outcomes of persuasion depend on how the arguments are structured, what should the nature of conclusion be, what choice of words should be used, and how to place the critical request in front of the audience. A speaker may be able to persuade his audiences if he designs a great message that has the power to change the beliefs and attitudes of his audiences. The speaker has to decide how he should package the message, organize his arguments, what to emphasize and what to avoid, which words to be used, and other issues concerning the appropriateness of the message.

We will consider three broad categories of message factors: the structure of the message, the content of the message, and the language employed in the message, which includes both words and symbols.

Structure of the Message

There are two areas that the speaker has to think through concerning the structure of the message. The first one is how the arguments should be ordered within the message, and the second one is how to conclude the message.

1. **Ordering of the arguments**: Every message is made up of a combination of arguments, some of which are more important for the overall outcome than are others. A common question frequently

asked is, should the most important argument be placed in the beginning of the message or in the end? A study of various speeches
showed that many speakers saved the best and most important argument for the last. Some speakers had a direct approach where they
put forward the most important argument at the beginning of the
message. It is also important to keep the context in mind to understand this well. Many contexts or situations where time is limited,
having the most important argument in the beginning as compared
to others is more impactful than having it at the end. Leaving aside
the context, experiments conducted on message structures showed
very little or marginal differences in the persuasive outcome when
the order or arguments were altered (Gilkinson, Paulson, & Sikkink,
1954). Other studies have focused on the effectiveness of using a
one-sided supportive perspective versus a two-sided pro and con
perspective. Results showed that speakers who presented two-sided
views and rejected the opposition view were more successful in persuading their audiences than those who ignored the opposing view
(Allen, 1998; Rucker, Petty, & Briñol, 2008). Audiences are willing
to change their attitudes more when they perceive the speaker to be
fair in mentioning and offering both sides of the argument and also
explaining why one side is stronger than the other.

2. **Positioning of the conclusion**: Another important aspect of the
   message structure is to have an explicit or implicit conclusion or
   recommendation for the audience. It has been seen repeatedly that
   messages with an explicit recommendation have more persuasive
   outcomes than a message without such features. An explicit recommendation also helps the audience to understand the message and
   comprehend the point better, though it may not necessarily result in
   a persuasive outcome (Thistlethwaite, Haan, & Kamenetzky, 1955).
   Two suggested strategies may be used for the conclusion. One is
   called the FITD or foot-in-the-door strategy where the message first
   includes a small request and then a larger or critical request. The
   underlying assumption here is that the audience will be more likely
   to be persuaded positively on the critical request if they have been
   positively persuaded on the first smaller request (Freedman & Fraser,
   1966). The second strategy is called the DITF, or door-in-the-face,

strategy, which consists of initially making a large request, which is usually turned down by the receiver, and then making a smaller critical request (Cialdini, et al., 1975).

Graham Hill's speech reflected a remarkable structuring of the message. Though his talk was very short and crisp, it gave a balanced view on the topic and included an effective conclusion:

So, please ask yourselves, for your health, for your pocketbook, for the environment, for the animals: What's stopping you from giving weekday veg a shot? After all, if all of us ate half as much meat, it would be like half of us were vegetarians.

Content of the Message

Many factors and variables of the message content affect the persuasive outcome:

- **Proof or evidence**: The term "evidence" can be thought of as factual data or information from a credible source that supports the claim of the message argument. Research has found that a message with evidence has a better persuasive impact than a message with no evidence (Reynolds & Reynolds, 2002). Some examples of the use of evidence in a message are facts, statistics, and testimonials. Studies suggest that examples are a powerful form of information as compared to information in a statistical summary form (Taylor & Thompson, 1982).
- **Case study, examples, or narratives**: A narrative, case study, or example is another way for a speaker to package the content and make it more persuasive for her audiences. A narrative is more interesting to audiences because it explains the situation in greater emotional detail than a statistical summary. Audiences tend to remember a story more than a number, and a narrative or case is more powerful than statistics or numbers in changing the attitudes of the audience.
- **Fear appeals**: Fear can be defined as an internal emotional reaction, which is experienced when the person perceives a personal threat

to his life or well-being. Fear can be a very good tool to bring out reactions in the audience. The technique is **also very commonly used in everyday** living, e.g., parents persuading children to give up candy because it will harm their teeth. Fear appeals are used in persuasive communication to produce a desired attitude change. Speakers can decide to choose a high fear appeal or a low fear appeal in their content. It has been seen that the messages that have a higher fear appeal are more persuasive than those with little or no fear appeal (Boster & Mongeau, 1984). Fear appeals might also produce a wrong effect if not chosen well. For instance, audiences might get turned off or deny to acknowledge the topic and its scariness. Another phenomenon that is commonly observed in audiences is that they may have either unrealistic optimism or the illusion of invulnerability, which means that bad things might happen to others but not to them, such as in the case of health and safety risks. One of the most popularly used frameworks to design a fear appeal in messages is the Extended Parallel Process Model (EPPM) by Kim Witte (Witte, 1998). The speaker must first elaborate on the problem by both offering the severity of the problem and the likelihood of the outcomes so that the audience is threatened. The speaker must then explain the solution and how the audience can apply the solution to themselves.

- **Guilt appeals**: Guilt is an emotional response like fear. It has similar properties to evoke attitude change in audiences. Speakers can choose the message content to infuse guilt in their audiences, making them feel that they have failed to do what they were supposed to do. The model explains that the speaker must outline a problem with which the audience can empathize. This explanation of the problem should arouse guilt in the audience and help them change their attitudes and take action to solve the problem. The best examples of such scenarios are charitable causes. In such cases a message strategy called EAPH (even a penny helps) is quite useful for those audiences who are not keen to participate and is typically used in fund-raising and money-collection campaigns (Cialdini & Schroeder, 1976).

In Graham Hill's speech, one can see flavors of these appeals used as evidence to prove the point he was trying to make:

The program has been great, weekday veg. My footprint's smaller, I'm lessening pollution, I feel better about the animals, I'm even saving money. Best of all, I'm healthier, I know that I'm going to live longer, and I've even lost a little weight.

Language Used in the Message

In the previous section, we examined the factors that make the content more persuasive. Another set of factors important to influencing audiences is related to language usage:

1. **Speed of speaking**: Though there is no concrete evidence that speed of speech enhances persuasive outcomes directly, there is evidence that it does have an indirect impact. Speaking fast can capture the attention of the audience at the beginning of the message. It can also gain attention when the speaker wants to add emphasis. Some audiences may perceive a fast speaker as nervous or insensitive toward the audience. A slow speed of speaking helps when the topics are sensitive or involve a large section of audiences with different cultural backgrounds, especially when they speak different languages. Overall, the study of speed of speech and persuasion is very complex and there is no clear evidence to suggest the right approach.

2. **Choice of words**: Many forms of linguistic study analyze the choice of words and their impact on the persuasive outcomes on audiences. While this is beyond the scope of this study, a few important factors are relevant for this study. Speakers who choose words that sound powerful are more successful in changing attitudes of their audiences as compared to those who chose words that undermine their power in the mind of the audience. Some examples of undermining language are hesitations, disclaimers, hedges, and tags. A prepared speaker who uses them less frequently is more likely to make a change in the audience. We have already considered the use of narratives and

stories as adding persuasive interest. Another aspect of power language that we will discuss a bit later is the use of metaphors.

3. **Intensity:** Messages with intense, strong words that are vivid and charged with emotions can be useful in bringing about persuasive outcomes in audiences. Studies show that intense words can have more impact on audiences under specific conditions that combine the credibility of the speaker, the involvement of the audience, and the appropriateness of the language (Hamilton & Hunter, 1998).

Graham Hill's speech had only 475 words, and he spoke for a little under 4 minutes. His speed was approximately 120 words per minute, which is considered ideal for public speaking. The choice of words was simple and easy to understand by any English speaking/understanding person in the world. He was not too forceful with his words. In fact, he used "I" sentences more than "you" sentences, which contradicts the Intensity point we examined, illustrating the point made that persuasive impact is often influenced by the scenario, context, and audience backgrounds.

Recipient/Audience Factors

The third part of the rhetoric triangle is the pathos or the state of the audience or recipient of the message. There are various characteristics of the recipient that can impact the persuasive outcome. This section will look at studies done in this regard.

The first recipient characteristic is the general and natural persuasibility of the recipient by the communicator or the message. Researchers have tried to answer the question, "are some people naturally more persuadable than others?" They have found that though some differences exist between recipients who are easily persuaded and those who aren't, the ease of persuasion is not that different between the two groups (Janis & Field, 1956). Some researchers have found that women in general are more persuadable than are men (Eagly & Carli, 1981). Some other personality traits to be aware of are the self-esteem of the recipient in relation to the persuasion message. If the recipient's self-esteem increases as a result of the message, there is a likely change in attitude and the persuasive outcome, though this is not always the case (Nisbett & Gordon, 1967).

The second characteristic that impacts a persuasive outcome is the inducement characteristic in the recipient. A simple explanation of this characteristic is the resistance of the recipient to be persuaded. Just as we inoculate children to make them less prone to diseases, similarly, researchers suggest that recipients can be inoculated with views that make them resistant to persuasion (McGuire, 1964).

The last set of audience factors we will consider are the contextual factors. In situations where the recipient and communicator are in a debate-like situation, the choice of who speaks first has a contextual effect on the persuasive outcome. The choice of medium also plays a crucial role, and researchers have seen that the same message that has a positive persuasive outcome on the recipients when delivered via a certain medium completely fails when sent through another medium (Mutz & Diana, 1988). Recipients are also impacted by the persistence of the message or the communicator and the timing of the message (Petty & Cacioppo, 1986).

The receiver factors will be examined from a different perspective in the next chapter, which describes the third lens of leadership theory.

Summary of the Factors That Impact the Persuasion Process

Table 4.1 summarizes the factors discussed in this chapter that impact success of the persuasion process.

Table 4.1 Summary of the factors that impact persuasion

Source factors	Message factors	Recipient factors
Expertise • Education, Occupation, Experience • Fluency in speaking • Personal position on the issue Trustworthiness • Likability • Similarity or kingship • Physical attractiveness • Style of delivery	Structure • Ordering of arguments • Positioning of conclusion Content • Evidence • Case/story/example • Fear Appeal • Guilt Appeal Language • Speed of speaking • Choice of words • Intensity of words	Personality Type • Inclination toward the topic • Resistance and longevity to persuasion Choice of medium

The factors that the lens of persuasion brings out now explain why some audiences will respond better to certain kind of messages and speaker. Again, these factors engage in interplay among themselves and emphasize the role of what is said and how it is said depending on the kind of the recipient. Political speeches often use this lens. Though persuasion is taught in many graduate and postgraduate schools, there is room to improve its application in the business and corporate context.

Both the lenses that have been covered in Chapters 3 and 4 focus more on the speaker and the message. Not much has yet been explained as to how the speaker or the message affects the followers. We will now try to understand this aspect from the third lens of our kaleidoscope. This lens of leadership theory is explained in the next chapter.

CHAPTER 5

The Third Lens— Charismatic Leadership

In previous chapters, lenses from theories of communication and persuasion were used to view the phenomena of successful public speaking. For both of these lenses, the factors of the sender and the message were explored in some detail. While in the last chapter, the concepts of understanding the receiver's beliefs, attitudes, and behaviors were discussed, the factors that really bring out the success of a message from a receiver's perspective will be explained in this chapter. This third lens from leadership studies completes the kaleidoscope of viewing the phenomena of impactful public speaking.

In this chapter, we will take the example of Susan Cain's TED talk that was delivered in February 2012. You can view the video here: http://www.ted.com/talks/susan_cain_the_power_of_introverts. Her speech on "The Power of Introverts" has been viewed more than 15 million times by audiences around the world. One of the more than 1,000 comments goes like this:

> This was a really inspiring and moving speech for me. I enjoy working in groups but always tell people my best ideas come when I am alone and to allow me to go away and reflect on things, it usually works but they get frustrated when I don't speak up. Introverts have lots to offer, sometimes more so than extroverts who often act on impulse without real consideration for the outcome. Thank you for your inspiring speech, it made me feel more comfortable in my skin.

Another viewer of this speech commented

She has brought me to tears.

What made these viewers feel like this? Because the theories from communication and persuasion may not be able to answer this question satisfactorily, this is where the theoretical lens of leadership studies, especially charisma, will help us have a better view of the phenomena.

What Is Leadership?

Leadership is a vast topic. Though the word "leader" first appeared in the English language in the year 1300, the word "leadership" did not appear until the first half of the nineteenth century (Bass, 2009). Historically, the theories of leadership and management were blurred. And while the two are interconnected, they began to be seen as separate realms of activity and research.

Leaders are not only supposed to think of the big picture but also perform a complex, intertwined combination of interpersonal, informational, and decisional roles (Mintzberg, 1975). By the 1970s, a new school of leadership studies emerged that distinguished leading from managing. It was argued that there are two types of leaders—transformational and transactional (Burns, 1978).

The transformational leader formulates the long-term objectives and vision, demonstrates transformational qualities of a leader, and influences a change in the values, attitudes, and behavior of others. The transactional leader engages in day-to-day activities and complies and supports the overall vision laid down by the transformational leader. In many ways, the transactional leader is a "manager" and the transformational leader is a "leader" (Conger & Kanungo, 1998). By the 1980s and 1990s, significant research in the area of Charismatic Leadership appeared, and the term Charismatic and Transformational were used interchangeably when describing leadership (Bryman, 1992, p. 10).

The Charismatic/Transformational Leader

The term charisma means a "gift." It is often used to define a person who is capable of having a profound and extraordinary effect on others and brings transformational effects on organizations and people (House & Baetz, 1979; Howell & Shamir, 2005).

German sociologist Max Weber's research identified specific attributes of charismatic leaders, which was carried forward by others who studied leadership qualities. Over time, two schools of thought emerged on charismatic leadership.

Some researchers believed that there are interconnected behavioral qualities of a charismatic leader that followers perceive and which make them follow the leader (Dow, 1969). According to this theory, charismatic leaders provided a strong emotion for the followers to identify with them so that they are influenced and inspired to follow a common goal, rethink their beliefs, and realize benefit to them (Bryman, 1992, p. 54).

But some researchers felt that charismatic leadership was not related to the personality of the leader. It was largely dependent on how they were perceived and appreciated by their followers (Willner, 1984). Some scholars including James Meindl (1990) criticized that the theory of charismatic leadership is too "leader-centered" and offered a "follower-oriented" approach. This approach takes the focus more toward how followers conceptualize leader behaviors and their potential impact (Meindl, 1990). It was felt that the charismatic effects are a function of social psychological forces operating among followers, subordinates, and observers, rather than arising directly out of the interactions between followers and leaders. Meindl argues that these forces are independent from the traits and behaviors of the leaders and hence the qualities of a leader are irrelevant in understanding charismatic leadership.

Both schools of thought have contributed to better understanding of charismatic leadership. Researchers now generally agree that they complement the subject instead of contradicting each other. There is no doubt that charismatic leadership is indeed an observable behavioral process that can be described and analyzed like any other leadership process between a leader and a follower. Goffee and Jones (2006) also suggest that this relationship depends a lot on the particular situation and the type of personalities of the leader and the followers (Goffee & Jones, 2006).

Researchers took this stream of research further and identified behavioral components that followers can observe to distinguish a charismatic leader from a noncharismatic leader. These traits included challenging the status quo, setting future goals, likability, trustworthiness, expertise, environmental sensitivity, articulation, and the ability to transform people. In other words, a charismatic leader advocates a cause and makes his follower believe in that cause. A key attribute relevant for our study is that a charismatic leader possesses strong articulation skills. As we move further in this study, we will now focus only on this aspect as the others are beyond the scope of the study.

Effects on Followers

Though a leader cannot survive without followers, it is very surprising that few studies have been done on the effects leaders have on followers as compared to studies focusing on leadership qualities. The best study comes from Shamir Boas, Robert House, and Michael Arthur, which will be used heavily in the following sections. Though the video of Susan Cain does not directly reflect leadership in action, it does serve as a case study to understand the theory better. Boas, House, and Arthur tried to explain what actually happens to followers especially as a result of the words spoken by the leader. The authors identified the following stages of follower response:

1. **Identification with the leader and the cause**: The followers tend to identify themselves with the leader. They start connecting their own values and beliefs to that of the leader and associate the leader's vision/mission to that of their own. The followers get a feeling that the leader is telling their story and understands exactly how they feel.
2. **High level of self-esteem and self-worth**: The followers feel elated, motivated, and inspired by the leader. They feel that they are important and are worthy of adding value to the cause. Feelings of low self-esteem and low self-worth are suppressed by the leader, giving rise to high levels of joy and happiness, which lead to heightened levels of motivation to continue on the path the leader has chosen.

3. **Personal commitment to the vision**: After listening to the leader, the followers get involved with the objective and the vision of the leader. If their own belief systems for the objective and the vision are similar, they are strengthened, and the followers become more committed toward both the leader and the vision. They also offer their own resources to make the vision a reality and spread the vision further to others.

4. **Meaningfulness in their life and work**: The followers feel that they are "somebody" in this world. They feel that they have a chance to make an impact and feel proud of what they are doing. The leader is able to connect the overall objective to the work of the followers and inspires them to find fulfillment in their own lives by following his vision. The leader gives them a reason to continue their journey and aligns them to his vision, which makes them think that they now have a purposeful and meaningful life.

5. **High levels of trust/likability/attraction toward the leader**: The followers feel attracted toward the leader. This attraction creates trust and likability of the leader, which is very evident in observing the followers of many charismatic leaders. Recently, I was watching a video clip of the current Indian prime minister Narendra Modi. The followers were spellbound by his words, were waving at him while shouting slogans. One could feel the palpable energy of this trust/likability/attraction effect in the video. This effect is also seen in the followers of spiritual leaders, celebrities, sport stars, artists, and so on.

Leader Rhetoric: A Behavioral Trait of Charismatic Leaders

Over the years, researchers have tried to establish strong linkages between persuasiveness of an individual and charismatic leadership. In order to be a successful advocate of a cause, a leader needs to be a persuasive and credible communicator. A charismatic leader will inspire his followers. The followers perceive a charismatic leader as an exciting public speaker—a skillful performer who is able to motivate and inspire individuals and groups, clearly convey his/her vision, articulate clear organizational goals, and provide new ideas for the future of the organization (Bryman, 1992; Conger & Kanungo, 1992).

Abraham Lincoln once said in a historical debate in 1858: "With public sentiment, nothing can fail; without it nothing can succeed. Consequently he who molds public sentiment goes deeper than he who enacts statutes or pronounces decisions" (Lincoln, Douglas, Davis, & Wilson, 2008).

So, overall, their seems to be support in literature and anecdotal evidence pointing to a strong link between the effectiveness of a leader and their communication skills. We can argue that to be a good leader, one must have strong communication skills to persuade others to action. So how do these charismatic leaders bring the desired effects on their followers? This field of study is still evolving but has seen some extraordinary breakthroughs among scholars. Shamir, House, and Arthur proposed a theory that links leader behavior and follower effects through follower self-concepts.

According to this linkage theory, a charismatic leader articulates his view to the followers by ensuring that some set of the followers' interests and values become congruent and complementary to those of the leader. The leader then becomes a role model by demonstrating various behaviors in line with the objective, which also increases the credibility of their message among the followers (Shamir, House, & Arthur, 1993). These effects on followers, which were explained in the preceding section, occur due to some specific steps, which we will now consider.

The first step involves the leader explaining to the followers the importance of the effort that is needed to fulfill the goal. This in turn makes the follower feel important, increases their self-worth, and causes them to feel needed. In the second step, the leader expresses confidence in the followers and highlights the importance of everyone's contribution toward the mission. In the next step, the leader explains how the mission has evolved over time, how it will benefit from the involvement of the followers, and how the collective group will be different from others. This helps the followers feel good about being a part of the collective movement. Next, the leader articulates the future, which will result in fulfillment of this mission and how it will make the lives of everyone better. And lastly, the leader encourages deeper commitment from followers toward the mission.

There are two ways that leaders achieve the above-mentioned purposes. The first one is that of *role modeling* in which the leader becomes a symbol of change, demonstrates qualities that are in line with the mission, leads from the front, and demonstrates visible changes of improvement to followers who then commit to the mission. The leader becomes a reference point for followers to emulate and learn from. Leaders such as Gandhi, Mandela, and King are very good examples of role models. Gandhi himself broke the salt law first. When he did so, thousands followed him and the British had no choice but to use violence and force. The resistance movement did not stop and, very soon, the law was changed. King's March on Selma was another example of role modeling. Mandela spent decades in prison and became the face of the apartheid movement in South Africa.

The second behavior by which the leader achieves the above-mentioned processes, which lead to the motivational effects in followers, is called *frame alignment*. As a part of this behavior, the words of the leader, his verbal and nonverbal communications, his style of delivery, and his overall behavior play a vital role.

Persuasion and communication are key processes that create this alignment between leaders and followers. Though much research has been done on the oratory aspect of speeches, it has not fully addressed charismatic leadership. Studies have focused more on the style rather than the content. One study of speeches of charismatic leaders did reveal a significant relationship between the rhetorical content of the speech and the charismatic impact on the followers (Shamir, House, & Arthur, 1994).

Some scholars such as Deane Hartog and Robert Verberg also argue that the relevance of charismatic leadership in international business strategy is very obvious and requires more attention on how the CEO is able to link the organization's strategy to the values of its the teams. This is an area of study deserving of further investigation. Broadly, it can be generalized that one of the most important qualities of a charismatic leader is to create rhetorical and persuasive messages for his followers (Hartog & Verburg, 1997).

It is argued that in order to bring the desired motivational effects to the audience, a speaker must make seven references in her speech.

I will now explain these references with examples of sentences from Susan Cain's TED talk.

1. **More references to history**: In a speech, a leader has to create a linkage from the past to the present so that the consistency of the mission can be seen by the followers. This will later set the ground for the leader to reveal a better future with the mission. This continuance creates a sense of evolution and progress in the minds of followers, which helps them understand the mission better. In Cain's talk, here are some sentences that she used, which follow this pattern:

   > Now in fact, some of our transformative leaders in history have been introverts. I'll give you some examples. Eleanor Roosevelt, Rosa Parks, Gandhi—all these peopled described themselves as quiet and soft-spoken and even shy. And they all took the spotlight, even though every bone in their bodies was telling them not to.

   Later she makes another reference to history in the sentence as reproduced below:

   > Even Carl Jung, the psychologist who first popularized these terms, said that there's no such thing as a pure introvert or a pure extrovert. He said that such a man would be in a lunatic asylum, if he existed at all. And some people fall smack in the middle of the introvert/extrovert spectrum, and we call these people ambiverts.

2. **More references to the collective and collective-identity**: Charismatic leaders use various references in their speech, which draw on the identity of the followers and the leader as part of a collective. Leaders can do this by referencing who they are, or where they come from, or from some common behavioral aspect that connects to the mission. These references cause the followers to feel drawn to the mission and help them realize that their individual presence is very important to the collective group and to the overall mission. A few instances where Cain used the collective identity of introverts and their problems are as follows:

   > A third to a half of the population are introverts—a third to a half. So that's one out of every two or three people you know.

So even if you're an extrovert yourself, I'm talking about your co-workers and your spouses and your children and the person sitting next to you right now—all of them subject to this bias that is pretty deep and real in our society. We all internalize it from a very early age without even having a language for what we're doing.

But then we hit the 20th century, and we entered a new culture that historians call the culture of personality. What happened is we had evolved from an agricultural economy to a world of big business. And so suddenly people are moving from small towns to the cities. And instead of working alongside people they've known all their lives, now they are having to prove themselves in a crowd of strangers.

3. **More positive references to followers' worth and efficacy**: To appeal to the interests of the followers, the leader will engage them by using words that make them feel worthy. She will try to bring out their qualities in her talk and connect these qualities to the importance of the mission. She will encourage the followers to build on these qualities and not feel that these qualities are not useful. Gradually, her words will make the followers feel that they are worthy and important to the mission. In Cain's talk, she gave various examples of how introverts are very important for the world and referred to famous leaders who were introverts as well. She did this to not only convince the introverts around the world realize that they are valuable, but also to boost their morale and motivate them for the mission that her talk outlined. She even used some credible research to back her arguments. Here is a sentence that illustrates the technique:

> An interesting research by Adam Grant at the Wharton School has found that introverted leaders often deliver better outcomes than extroverts do, because when they are managing proactive employees, they're much more likely to let those employees run with their ideas, whereas an extrovert can, quite unwittingly, get so excited about things that they're [sic] putting their own stamp on things, and other people's ideas might not as easily then bubble up to the surface.

4. **More references to the speaker's similarity to audience's**: A leader has to make the followers feel that she is like them and is part of their collective group. She does this by pointing out similarities between herself and her followers, which could be based on a variety of factors such as experience, language, culture, backgrounds, education, etc. The leader becomes a representative of this collective group, which the followers connect with better and then emulate her views because of the similarities.

    Here are some references to this technique in Cain's talk.

    Now, I tell you this story about summer camp. I could have told you 50 others just like it—all the times that I got the message that somehow my quiet and introverted style of being was not necessarily the right way to go, that I should be trying to pass as more of an extrovert. And I always sensed deep down that this was wrong and that introverts were pretty excellent just as they were. But for years I denied this intuition, and so I became a Wall Street lawyer, of all things, instead of the writer that I had always longed to be—partly because I needed to prove to myself that I could be bold and assertive, too. And I was always going off to crowded bars when I really would have preferred to just have a nice dinner with friends. And I made these self-negating choices so reflexively, that I wasn't even aware that I was making them.

5. **More references to values and moral justifications**: Charismatic leaders try to raise the followers' values to higher levels of principles and morals. This is also a key differentiating factor between transformational and transactional leaders. In their talk, leaders use arguments from morality and ethics to explain the situation and engage the followers to raise their own moral standards for a larger collective mission. These flavors are often seen in political leaders' speeches. But there are subtle observations on this reference type in Cain's talk as well. She appeals to the audience on the importance of working together in an organization but then questions whether it is the best way for the introverts. She questions the education system where children are made to sit in pods or groups and encouraged to learn

together as opposed to the older system where each child would learn on his or her own. She also talks about the importance of spending time alone and being in solitude and gives examples of leaders seen as principled and moral.

> Okay, number two: Go to the wilderness. Be like Buddha, have your own revelations. I'm not saying that we all have to now go off and build our own cabins in the woods and never talk to each other again, but I am saying that we could all stand to unplug and get inside our own heads a little more often.

6. **More references to long-term goals and future**: A leader explains how the future will change if her mission is implemented. She also outlines the steps to make this happen for the followers. The followers are able to see a clear impact through her words and are able to implement the steps toward the mission. The followers can also analyze and understand what will happen if the leader's mission is not implemented and how it will impact them as well. They feel motivated to implement the mission because they also see a direct benefit to themselves.

In Cain's talk, she outlines three steps for followers to implement her mission. She also outlines how the workplace can be improved if introverts are allowed their space and freedom to work alone. She also clearly outlines that she is not against working in teams. But she urges everyone to recognize the power that introverts bring to the workplace and outlines a way to capitalize on it:

> Now none of this is to say that social skills are unimportant, and I'm also not calling for the abolishing of teamwork at all. The same religions who send their sages off to lonely mountain tops also teach us love and trust. And the problems that we are facing today in fields like science and in economics are so vast and so complex that we are going to need armies of people coming together to solve them working together. But I am saying that the more freedom that we give introverts to be themselves, the more likely that they are to come up with their own unique solutions to these problems.

7. **More references to hope and faith**: Leaders motivate their followers by raising their hopes and increasing their faith in the mission. This is again seen more commonly in political speeches and only in a veiled way in Cain's talk. Though she mentions the word hope three times in her speech, she doesn't mention faith directly. Given the nature of this talk and its relevance to the audiences, it is understandable that mentions of hope and faith are minimal as compared to speeches from political leaders:

> But I'll tell you, what helps even more is my sense, my belief, my hope that when it comes to our attitudes to introversion and to quiet and to solitude, we truly are poised on the brink of dramatic change. I mean, we are. And so I am going to leave you now with three calls for action for those who share this vision.

Summary of the Factors That Impact the Communication Process from the Leadership Theories

Table 5.1 summarizes the factors of a communication process as we have discussed and as defined in literature of leadership studies.

Table 5.1 Summary of factors that impact communication from a leadership perspective

Sender	Message	Recipient
1. Charismatic qualities such as challenging the status quo, setting a future goal, likability, trustworthiness, expertise, environmental sensitivity, articulation and being able to transform people 2. Role modeling 3. Frame alignment	More references to: 1. History 2. Collective and collective-identity 3. Follower's worth and efficacy 4. Speaker's similarity to that of audience 5. Values and moral justifications 6. Long-term goals and future 7. Hope and faith	1. Followership effects and increase in self-worth 2. Attraction for leader 3. Heightened levels of motivation 4. Raise in self-belief 5. Commitment toward the mission from the leader

These leadership factors support and strengthen the factors that the communication and persuasion studies brought out earlier. The most important gap that this lens of leadership theory fulfills is how the recipients are motivated to follow the actions proposed by the speaker. Unless the recipients feel a deep sense of commitment toward the speaker and the mission, they will not agree and support the same. And for them to be committed, they should not only agree with the logic of the mission and the benefits it brings them as the theory of persuasion explains, they should also feel a heightened sense of self-esteem and self-worth by joining the mission. In addition, they should sense that the speaker is making them feel important for the mission and are attracted by his personality, character, background, beliefs, appearance, and style.

With this, we now have covered all the three lenses individually. It is time to put them all together and define the public speaking kaleidoscope.

CHAPTER 6

The Public Speaking Kaleidoscope

Putting It All Together

Chapters 1 and 2 gave us a multifaceted perspective on why some speeches are more impactful than others. In Chapter 3, 4, and 5, we outlined three theoretical lenses of public speaking. In this chapter, these lenses will be combined to create the kaleidoscope. This will help provide understanding of the effectiveness of particular speeches and strategies for creating speeches with maximum impact.

The Public Speaking Kaleidoscope

The Public Speaking Kaleidoscope has three lenses as shown in Figure 6.1. The first lens is from the theory of communication, which focuses on *sharing* with an audience. The second lens is taken from the theory of persuasion and focuses on bringing a *change* in audiences. The last lens is taken from the theory of charismatic leadership and focuses on *leading* an audience.

We will apply what we have learned about each lens and consider the interactions of the three elements in creating impactful speeches.

Lessons from the Lens of Communication Theory: Sharing with an Audience

In Chapter 3, we saw that communication theory identifies the following elements of public speaking: sender, cues, meaning, message, channel, and receiver. The theory provides many insights into each of these

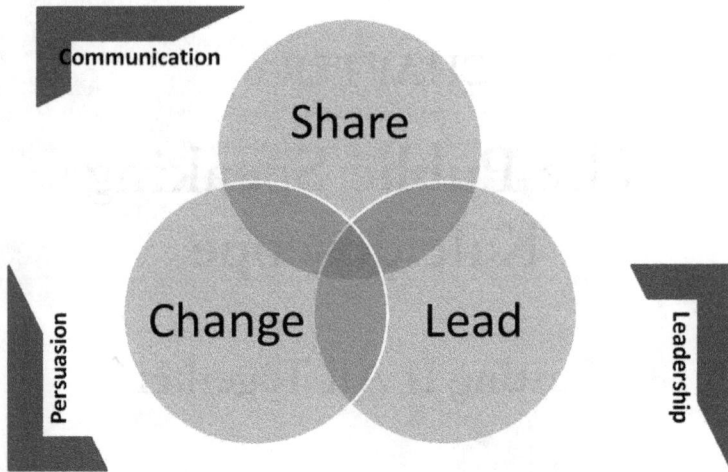

Figure 6.1 The Public Speaking Kaleidoscope: Three lenses that explain why some speeches are more impactful than others

elements, which helps us understand what constitutes an impactful speech. Broadly, what the theory reckons significant are the dimensions of the sender and the message, and the distortions that can result because of the channel, cues, and meaning. The strongest aspect of this model is that it emphasizes the communication competence of the sender and blends all the other aspects of creating a message and understanding the recipient as responsibilities of the sender. This theory looks at the process of the communication and does not focus specifically on public speaking. The same model can be applied to a conversation in a meeting room, a gossip session at the water-cooler, or a telephone chat between parties located in separate countries.

Lessons from the Lens of Persuasion Theory: Changing an Audience

In Chapter 4, we saw how the persuasion theory outlines public speaking into the following elements: source factors, message factors, and recipient factors. The gaps of the communication theory were addressed by the persuasion theory. Persuasion is considered as a tool or a means to bring about a change. This lens provides a rich view of how audience attitudes and beliefs play a vital role in the impact of the message. In addition, this theory specifically addresses public speaking. The theory's most significant strength is the depth it provides in understanding message creation for a particular audience.

Lessons from the Lens of Charismatic Leadership: Leading an Audience

In Chapter 5, we saw how the theory of charismatic leadership applies to the basic elements of public speaking: sender, message, and recipient. We also examined the effects of charismatic leadership on followers in greater detail. This final lens provides the missing link to understanding audience impact by emphasizing the impact of the leader's communication on followers.

Putting It All Together

The Public Speaking Kaleidoscope reveals the following characteristics.

Qualities of the Source/Speaker

The credibility of the speaker and his ability or competence to think, create, and deliver the message is clearly a very important quality that has impact on audiences. Skills and behaviors in this area include the following:

1. Confidence of the speaker
2. Energy
3. Belief and sincerity in the topic
4. Tone
5. Diction
6. Vocal variety
7. Speed
8. Gestures
9. Movements
10. Eye contact

11. Facial expressions
12. Posture
13. Handling audience questions
14. Understanding audience
15. Role modeling
16. Track record/credibility
17. Challenging status quo
18. Transformational appeal
19. Appearance/physical attractiveness
20. Kinship with audience

Qualities of the Message

The various qualities of the message that make an impact on the audiences as per the three lenses include the following:

1. Person-centered message
2. Verbal and nonverbal elements
3. Push or pull (influencing or shaping)
4. Structure
   a. Ordering of arguments
   b. Positioning of conclusion
5. Content
   a. Evidence
   b. Case/story/example
   c. Fear appeal
   d. Guilt appeal
6. Language
   a. Speed of speaking
   b. Choice of words
   c. Intensity of words
7. References to
   a. History
   b. Collective and collective-identity
   c. Followers' worth and efficacy
   d. Speaker's similarity to the audience

   e. Values and moral justifications

   f. Long-term goals and future

   g. Hope and faith

Qualities of the Recipient

Lastly, the various qualities of the recipient include the following:

1. Maturity
2. Involvement
3. Interpersonal cognitive complexity
4. Personality type
5. Inclination toward the topic
6. Resistance and longevity to persuasion
7. Choice of medium
8. Followership effects and increase in self-worth
9. Attraction for leader
10. Heightened levels of motivation
11. Increase in self-belief
12. Commitment toward the mission and the leader

As we can see, the Public Speaking Kaleidoscope brings out more than 50 dimensions that influence the speech process. These 50+ dimensions engage in interplay with one another and can have millions of permutations and combinations, depending on the behavior of the sender and receiver. This explains why each of us can have a very different interpretation and attitude toward a speaker and why the impact on the audience can vary from person to person.

Analyzing the Gettysburg Address Using Our Kaleidoscope

In the first chapter, we discussed Abraham Lincoln's famous Gettysburg address. Let us now see how the Public Speaking Kaleidoscope helps us in understanding the impact of this speech. Given that this speech has no video recording, we must rely on how historians have recorded the event. It is said that Abraham Lincoln read from a paper at the very somber occasion. So the communication competence and delivery style of Abraham Lincoln may not have had much impact on the audience. But the words of the message seemed to have qualities of a "person-centered" message and captured the feelings of the society of that time. It was a short speech—only 272 words. But these words were so well-crafted and structured together that the effect it had on the listeners was very moving and motivational. The speech reflected the qualities identified in charismatic leadership theory: references to history, values, hope, and a better future. Audiences of this speech, even until today, experience an increase in their own self-beliefs, self-worth, and commitment to the cause of democracy.

We can apply the same exercise to any speech and explore how and why it has impact. The kaleidoscope, for instance, can explain why the speech of Donald Trump, the 45th president of USA, has impact. If one analyzes his delivery style, he uses very repetitive words such as "fantastic," "great," "huge," and other words that some critics of speechwriting might frown upon. His face usually has a frown and often and expression of arrogance. He barely smiles and uses pointed hand gestures, which, again, might not be perceived as appropriate by many audiences.

So why is Donald Trump able to have such an impact? There could be a few possible answers to that as revealed by the kaleidoscope. First, the audiences who are impacted positively by Donald Trump might like his arrogance and his directness. Deep inside, they might have resented that their jobs have been given to non-Americans. Deep inside, they were unhappy with the way the world was progressing and leaving them behind. And now here is a leader who is speaking their language. Their own anger is coming out through his words, and they feel a great sense of commitment toward someone who understands their plight.

What excites me most these days is that despite having so many theories, we still haven't fully figured out what really works in public speaking. Abraham Lincoln and Donald Trump are two extremes of a spectrum when viewed from this kaleidoscope, yet both have impacted a wide following.

The Road Ahead

Now that you have read this book, you hopefully can apply the information in several ways as follows.

A Tool to Measure the Quality of Public Speaking

This book has presented a kaleidoscope with 50+ dimensions that explain public speaking impact. Application of this tool can assist you in improving your own public speaking. You can extend each dimension on a five-point scale and perform a self-analysis on each characteristic. You can also ask for input from friends or colleagues to rate you on each dimension after listening to your speech. This process can then become an ongoing measurement mechanism for you to gauge progress with every speaking activity. A sample tool is provided in Appendix A at the end of this book.

A Roadmap for Future Academic Work on This Topic

This study is just a tiny drop in the large ocean of communication studies. There are many new areas where the literature can be renewed or expanded with new research. Potential areas for study include the following:

1. **The importance of emotions and how to analyze them from a perspective of a message, a speaker, or an audience.** The TED platform can capture some emotional responses from the comments that are posted by those who view the videos. While emotions are individually experienced and very difficult to measure, studies could use a combination of qualitative and quantitative techniques to record the emotional impact of communication.

2. **The role of new media in persuasion.** With Internet, laptops, cell phones, and tablets, communication happens more and more through technological channels. The last several years have seen an explosion in the use of new media with social platforms such as Twitter, Facebook, and LinkedIn and educational platforms such as Coursera and Udacity. Adapting the communication framework to reflect the complexities of new media is an area that can be explored in the future.

3. **The interplay of the relationships with the themes and the dimensions of communication, persuasion, and leadership.** Given that this study has revealed 50+ dimensions that can be measured, a few key factors can be taken and analyzed as to how they work

together for a given scenario. An example of this could be how aspects of the three elements impact audience bias and acceptance of the overall message. Another example could be to find out how much delivery style impacts an audience in business scenarios where content is more important. Such a study could be beneficial to presenters who cannot overcome their fear of public speaking but are able to structure the message quite well. Many other possibilities for similar further research exist.

4. **How the kaleidoscope elements apply to various cultures.** Many of the academic theories were developed by Americans and published in American journals. Additional research might be conducted that takes those frameworks and explores their relevance in other cultural contexts. For instance, an interesting model called the "sadharani-karan" model of Hindu communication has been discussed in a few universities in India and Nepal. A joint effort between Indian and Western researchers could be made to combine these frameworks to better understand the cultural dynamics of communication in a globalized world.

5. **Analysis of business speeches from different cultures.** Application of qualitative methods and grounded theory methods can be utilized in a variety of other similar studies such as speech analysis of business leaders from various cultures. There are plenty of such studies that have been done on speeches of political leaders of the world. The best practices can be used for local scenarios.

6. **Application of software tools to analyze content.** Currently there are tools available such as LIWC—Linguistic Inquiry and Word Count (LIWC, 2015). An example of using LIWC would be to study how certain words are more persuasive than others and how audiences react to certain words in emails. The study can then result in the creation of a tool that can help a corporate manager to select words that are more suited for a message as compared to others. A software tool might also be created to track other parameters discussed in this book and analyze those for communication enhancement.

7. **Curriculum design.** The frameworks and theories used in the study can be helpful in designing curriculum for various technical and

business colleges. In the corporate world, training modules can be created to help managers overcome their fears of facing an audience and improve their communication skills.

8. **Cross-disciplinary collaboration.** The subject of communication spans many disciplines. In schools of management, this topic is ripe for collaboration with a variety of other disciplines and departments including marketing communication, consumer behavior, decision making, leadership, organizational behavior, human resources, and many more.

9. **Discipline expansion.** Finally, such study can result in research papers, articles, books, and cases that can be useful to both academic scholars and practitioners.

Sample Tool to Measure Effectiveness of Public Speaking

Quality of the Speaker	Excellent	Good	Average	Poor	Very Poor
Confidence of the speaker					
Energy					
Belief and sincerity in the topic					
Tone					
Diction					
Vocal variety					
Speed					
Gestures					
Movements					
Eye contact					
Facial expressions					
Posture					
Handling audience questions					
Understanding audience					
Role modeling					

Quality of the Speaker	Excellent	Good	Average	Poor	Very Poor
Track record/ credibility					
Challenging status quo					
Transformational appeal					
Appearance/Physical attractiveness					
Kinship with audience					

Quality of the Message	Excellent	Good	Average	Poor	Very Poor
Person-centered message					
Verbal and non-verbal elements					
Push or pull (influencing or shaping)					
Structure					
Ordering of arguments					
Positioning of conclusion					
Content					
Evidence					
Case/story/example					
Fear appeal					
Guilt appeal					
Language					
Speed of speaking					
Choice of words					
Intensity of words					
References to history					
References to collective and collective-identity					
References to followers' worth and efficacy					
References to speaker's similarity to the audience					
References to values and moral justifications					
References to long-term goals and future					
References to hope and faith					

Quality of the Recipient	Excellent	Good	Average	Poor	Very Poor
Maturity					
Involvement					
Interpersonal cognitive complexity					
Personality type					
Inclination toward the topic					
Resistance and longevity to persuasion					
Choice of medium					
Followership effects and increase in self-worth					
Attraction for leader					
Heightened levels of motivation					
Increase in self-belief					
Commitment toward the mission and the leader					

Bibliography

Abramson, P. R., Rohde, J. H. & Aldrich, D. W. (2009). *Change and continuity in the 2008 elections*. Washington, DC: CQ Press.

Adhikary, N. M. (2009). An introduction to sadharanikaran model of communication. *Bodhi: An Interdisciplinary Journal, 3*(1), 69–91.

Allen, M. (1998). Comparing the persuasive effectiveness of one and two sided messages. In M. Allen, & R. W. Preiss (Eds.), *Persuasion: Advance through metaanalysis* (pp. 87–98). New York, NY: Hampton Press.

Andersen, K., & Clevenger, T. (1963). A summary of experimental research in ethos. *Communications Monographs, 30*(2), 59–78.

Anderson, N. H. (1965). Averaging versus adding as a stimulus-combination rule in impression formation. *Journal of Experimental Psychology, 70*(4), 394.

Antonakis, J., Fenley, M., & Liechti, S. (2011). Can charisma be taught? Tests of two interventions. *Academy of Management Learning & Education, 10*(3), 374–396.

Bandiera, O., Guiso, L., Prat, A., & Sadun, R. (2011). *What do CEOs do?* Boston, MA: Harvard Business School.

Barnlund, D. C. (2008). A transactional model of communication. In C. D. Mortensen (Ed.), *Communication theory* (pp. 47–57). New Brunswic, NJ: Transaction Publishers.

Bass, B. M. (2009). *Bass handbook of leadership: Theory, research & managerial applications* (4th ed.). New York, NY: Free Press.

Bass, B. M., & Avolio, B. J. (1993). Transformational leadership and organizational culture. *Public Administration Quarterly, 17*(1), 112–120.

Beisecker, T. D., & Parson, D. W. (1972). *The process of social influence: readings in persuasion* (1st ed.). New York, NY: Prentice-Hall.

Belliotti, R. A. (2009). *Niccolo Machiavelli: The laughing lion and the strutting fox.* Plymouth, England: Lexington Books.

Berlo, D. K. (1960). *The process of communication.* New York, NY: Holt, Reinehart & Winston.

Berlo, D. K., Lemert, J. B., & Mertz, R. J. (1969). Dimensions for evaluating the acceptability of message sources. *Public Opinion Quarterly, 33*(4), 563–576.

Boster, F. J., & Mongeau, P. (1984). Fear-arousing persuasive messages. In: R. N. Bostrom (Ed.), *Communication yearbook* (Vol. 8, pp. 330–375). Beverly Hills, CA: Sage.

Brock, T. (1965). Communicator-recipient similarity and decision change. *Journal of Personality and Social Psychology, 1*, 650–654.

Bromme, R., Rambow, R., & Nückles, M. (2001). Expertise and estimating what other people know: The influence of professional experience and type of knowledge. *Journal of Experimental Psychology: Applied, 7*(4), 317–330.

Bryman, A. (1992). *Charisma and leadership in organizations.* London, England: Sage.

Burgoon, J. K., & Poire, L. (1993). Effects of communication expectancies, actual communication, and expectancy disconfirmation on evaluations of communicators and their communication behavior. *Human Communication Research, 20*(1), 67–96.

Burgoon, J. K., Buller, D. B., Dillman, L., & Walther, J. B. (1995). Interpersonal deception. *Human Communication Research, 22*(2), 163–196.

Burleson, B. R. (2010). Constructivism: A general theory of communication skill. In B. Whaley, & W. Samter (Eds.), *Explaining communication: Theory and examplars* (pp. 109–112). New York, NY: Routeledge.

Burleson, B. R., Delia, J. G., & Applegate, J. L. (1992). Effects of maternal communication and children's social-cognitive and communication skills on children's acceptance by the peer group. *Family Relations, 41*, 264–272.

Burns, J. (1978). *Leadership.* New York, NY: Harper Collins.

Carlyle, T. (1993). *On heroes, hero-worship, and the heroic in history* (Vol. 1). Oakland, CA: Univ of California Press.

Cialdini, R. B. (2001). Harnessing the science of persuasion. *Harvard Business Review, 79*(9), 72–81.

Cialdini, R. B., & Schroeder, D. A. (1976). Increasing compliance by legitimizing paltry contributions: When even a penny helps. *Journal of Personality and Social Psychology, 34*(4), 599–604.

Cialdini, R. B., Vincent, J. E., Lewis, S. K., Catalan, J., Wheeler, D., & Darby, B. L. (1975). Reciprocal concessions procedure for inducing compliance: The door-in-the-face technique. *Journal of Personality and Social Psychology, 31*(2), 206–215.

Cicero, M. T. (1960). *De Inventione* (H. M. Hubbell, Trans.). Cambridge, MA: Harvard University Press.

Clark, R. A., & Delia, J. G. (1979). Topoi and rhetorical competence. *Quarterly Journal of Speech, 65*(2), 187–206.

Conger, J. A. (1998). The necessary art of persuasion. *Harvard Business Review, 76*(3), 84–95.

Conger, J. A., & Kanungo, R. N. (1987). Toward a behavioral theory of charismatic leadership in organizational settings. *Academy of Management Review, 12*(4), 637–647.

Conger, J. A., & Kanungo, R. N. (1992). Perceived behavioural attributes of charismatic leadership. *Canadian Journal of Behavioral Science, 26*(1), 860102.

Conger, J. A., & Kanungo, R. N. (1998). *Charismatic leadership in organizations* (pp. 7–9). London, England: Sage.

Cooper, J., Darley, J. M., & Henderson, J. E. (1974). On the effectiveness of deviant-and conventional-appearing communicators: A field experiment. *Journal of Personality and Social Psychology, 29*(6), 752–757.

Dance, F. E. (1970). The "concept" of communication. *Journal of Communication, 20*(2), 201–210.

Doherty, M. E., & Kurz, E. M. (1996). Social judgement theory. *Thinking & Reasoning, 2*(2-3), 109–140.

Dow, T. E. (1969). The theory of charisma. *Sociological Quarterly, 10*(3), 306–318.

Eagly, A. H., & Carli, L. L. (1981). Sex of researchers and sex-typed communications as determinants of sex differences in influenceability: a meta-analysis of social influence studies. *Psychological Bulletin, 90*(1), 1–20.

Eagly, A. H., & Chaiken, S. (1975). An attribution analysis of the effect of communicator characteristics on opinion change: The case of communicator attractiveness. *Journal of Personality and Social Psychology, 32*(1), 136–144.

Eagly, A. H., Wood, W., & Chaiken, S. (1978). Causal inferences about communicators and their effect on opinion change. *Journal of Personality and Social Psychology, 36*(4), 424.

Federman, M. (2004, July 23). *What is the meaning of the medium is the message?* Retrieved from http://individual.utoronto.ca/markfederman/article_mediumisthemessage.htm

Fishbein, M. (1991). *Readings in attitude theory and measurement.* UMI Books on Demand.

Freedman, J. L., & Fraser, S. C. (1966). Compliance without pressure: the foot-in-the-door technique. *Journal of Personality and Social Psychology, 4*(2), 195–202.

Gagarin, M. (2001). Did the sophists aim to persuade? *Rhetorica: A Journal of the History of Rhetoric, 19*(3), 275–291.

Gilkinson, H., Paulson, S. F., & Sikkink, D. E. (1954). Effects of order and authority in an argumentative speech. *Quarterly Journal of Speech, 40*(2), 183–192.

Godhwani, R. (2014). *What to Say and When to Shut Up.* India: Random House, 12–15.

Goethals, G. R., & Nelson, E. R. (1973). Similarity in the influence process: The belief-value distinction. *Journal of Personality and Social Psychology, 25*(1), 117–122.

Goffee, R., & Jones, G. (2006). *Why should anyone be led by you?: What it takes to be an authentic leader.* Boston, MA: Harvard Business Press.

Greenberg, J. H. (1966). *Universals of language.* Boston, MA: MIT.

Hamilton, M. A., & Hunter, J. E. (1998). The effect of language intensity on receiver evaluations of message, source, and topic. In M. Allen, & R. W. Preiss (Eds.), *Persuasion: Advances through meta-analysis* (pp. 99–138). Cresskill, NJ: Hampton Press.

Harmon-Jones, E. (2002). A cognitive dissonance theory perspective on persuasion. In J. P. Dillard, & L. Shen (Eds.), *The persuasion handbook: Developments in theory and practice* (pp. 99–116.). Thousands Oak, CA: Sage.

Hartog, D. N., & Verburg, R. M. (1997). Charisma and rhetoric: Communicative techniques of international business leaders. *Leadership Quarterly, 8*(4), 355–391.

Hewes, D. E. (1995). Cognitive processing of problematic messages: Reinterpreting to "unbias" texts. In D. E. Hewes (Ed.), *The cognitive bases of interpersonal communication* (pp. 113–138). Hillsdale, NJ: Lawrence Erlbaum Associates.

House, R. J., & Baetz, M. L. (1979). Leadership: Some empirical generalizations and new research directions. *Research in Organizational Behavior, 1*, 340–341.

House, R. J., Spangler, W. D., & Woycke, J. (1991). Personality and charisma in the U.S. presidency: A psychological theory of leader effectiveness. *Administrative Science Quarterly, 36*(3), 364–396.

Howell, J. M., & Shamir, B. (2005). The role of followers in the charismatic leadership process: Relationships and their consequences. *Academy of Management Review, 30*(1), 96–112.

Huebner, T. S. (2013). *How Lincoln's Gettysburg Address changed the nation.* Retrieved October 1, 2014, from http://www.marketwatch.com/story/how-lincoln-changed-the-nation-in-272-words-2013-11-19

Huebner, T. S., & DeRosa, M. L. (1993). The Confederate Constitution of 1861: An inquiry into American constitutionalism. *The Florida Historical Quarterly, 4*(71), 508–510.

Jamieson, K. H., & Campbell, K. K. (1982). Rhetorical hybrids: Fusions of generic elements. *Quarterly Journal of Speech, 68*(2), 146–157.

Janis, I. L., & Field, P. B. (1956). A behavioral assessment of persuasibility: Consistency of individual differences. *Sociometry, 19*, 241–259.

Katriel, T. (1986). *Talking straight: Dugri speech in Israeli Sabra culture.* Cambridge, England: Cambridge University Press.

Kennedy, G. A. (1991). *On Rhetoric: A theory of civic discourse.* Oxford, England: Oxford University Press.

Kiparsky, P. (1994). [Ashtadhyayi].*The Encyclopedia of Language and Linguistics* (6 ed.).

Knowledge@Wharton (2012). *Knowledge@Wharton.* [Online] Retrieved August 10, 2014 from: http://knowledge.wharton.upenn.edu/article/indias-new-hr-challenge-managing-multigenerational-workforce/.

Lannamann, J. W. (1991). Interpersonal communication research as ideological practice. *Communication Theory, 1*(3), 179–203.

Lasswell, H. (1971). *Propaganda technique in the world war.* Cambridge, MA: MIT Press.

Latha, K. (2013). Smart CEO of the business Samrajya: Management views from Kautilya's Arthasastra. *Effective Executive, 16*(4), 29.

Lincoln, A. (2009). *The gettysburg address.* London, England: Penguin.

Lincoln, A., Douglas, S. A., Davis, R. O., & Wilson, D. L. (2008). *The Lincoln-Douglas debates.* Champaign, IL: University of Illinois Press.

LIWC. (2015). *LIWC.* Retrieved from http://liwc.wpengine.com/

Lucas, K., & Rawlins, J. D. (2015). The competency pivot introducing a revised approach to the business communication curriculum. *Business and Professional Communication Quarterly, 78*(2), 1–27.

Maddux, J. E., & Rogers, R. W. (1980). Effects of source expertness, physical attractiveness, and supporting arguments on persuasion: A case of brains over beauty. *Journal of Personality and Social Psychology, 39*(2), 234–244.

Mahambre, V., & Nadkarni, R. (2011). *Crisil report: Employment in India.* Mumbai, India: Crisil.

McCroskey, J. C. (2006). Reliability and validity of the generalized attitude measure and generalized belief measure. *Communication Quarterly, 54*(3), 265–274.

McCroskey, J. C., & Mehrley, S. R. (1969). The effects of disorganization and nonfluency on attitude change and source credibility. *Communications Monographs, 36*(1), 13–21.

McGuire, W. J. (1964). Inducing resistance to persuasion: Some Contemporary approaches. *Advances in Experimental Social Psychology, 1*, 191–229.

McWhorter, J. (2011). *The power of Babel: A natural history of language* (1st ed.). New York, NY: Random House.

Mehrabian, A. (2008). Communication without words. In C. D. Mortensen (Ed.), *Communication Theory* (2nd ed., pp. 193–200). New Brunswick, NJ: Transaction.

Meindl, J. (1990). On Leadership: An alternative to the conventional wisdom. *Research in Organizational Behavior, 12*, 159–203.

Mills, J., & Kimble, C. E. (1973). Opinion change as a function of perceived similarity of the communicator and subjectivity of the issue. *Bulletin of the Psychonomic Society, 2*(1), 35–36.

Mintzberg, H. (1973). *The nature of managerial work.* New York, NY: Harper & Row.

Mintzberg, H. (1975). The managers job folklore and fact. *Harvard Business Review, 53*(4), 49–61.

Mintzberg, H. (2009). *Managing* (p. 9). San Francisco, CA: Berret-Koehler.

Mutz, S. H., & Diana, C. C. (1988). Comparing mediated and interpersonal communication data. In R. P. Hawkins, J. M. Wiemann, & S. Pingree (Eds.), *Advancing communication science: Merging mass and interpersonal processes* (pp. 19–43). Riverside, CA: Sage.

Nisbett, R. E., & Gordon, A. (1967). Self-esteem and susceptibility to social influence. *Journal of Personality and Social Psychology, 5*(3), 268–276.

O'Keefe, D. J. (1990a). Message factors. In D. J. O'Keefe (Ed.), *Persuasion: Theory and research* (pp. 158–174). Newbury Park, CA: Sage.

O'Keefe, D.J. (1990b). Source factors. In D. J. O'Keefe (Ed.), *Persuasion Theory and Research* (pp. 131–155). Newbury Park, CA: Sage.

Peters, B., & Nielsen, R. K. (2013). New media. In P. Simonson, J. Peck, R. T. Craig, & J. P. Jackson (Eds.), *The handbook of communication history* (pp. 257–267). New York, NY: Routeledge.

Petty, R. E., Priester, J. R., & Brinol, P. (2009). Mass media attitude change: Implications of the elaboration likelihood model of persuasion. In J. Bryant, & M. B. Oliver (Eds.), *Media effects: Advances in theory and research* (pp. 155–198). New York, NY: Routeledge.

Petty, R., & Cacioppo, J. T. (1986). *Communication and persuasion: Central and peripheral routes to attitude change.* New York, NY: Springer-Verlag.

Radicati, S. (2013). *Email statistics report, 2013–2017.* Palo Alto, CA: The Radicati Group.

Reinard, J. C. (1988). The empirical study of the persuasive effects of evidence the status after fifty years of research. *Human Communication Research, 15*(1), 3–59.

Reinard, J. C. (1991). Foundations of argument. In W. C. Brown, & D. Zarefsky (Eds.), *Effective communication for critical thinking* (p. 102). Dubuque, IA: William C. Brown.

Reynolds, R. A., & Reynolds, L. J. (2002). Evidence. In J. P. Dillard, & L. Shen (Eds.), *The persuasion handbook: Developments in theory and practice* (pp. 427–444). Thousand Oaks, CA: Sage.

Rhys, R. W. (2004). *Aristotle rhetoric trans.* Mineola, NY: Dover Publications.

Rinke, E. M., & Röder, M. (2011). The Arab Spring: Media ecologies, communication culture, and temporal-spatial unfolding: Three components in a communication model of the Egyptian regime change. *International Journal of Communication, 5*, 13.

Rogers, C. R., & Roethlisberger, F. J. (1991). Barriers and gateways to communication. *Harvard Business Review, 69*(6), 105–111.

Rogers, E. M. (1997). *A history of communication study: A biographical approach.* New York, NY: Free Press.

Rucker, D. D., Petty, R. E., & Briñol, P. (2008). What's in a frame anyway?: A meta-cognitive analysis of the impact of one versus two sided message framing on attitude certainty. *Journal of Consumer Psychology, 18*(2), 137–149.

Sacks, H. (1992). *Lectures on conversation.* Cambridge, MA: Blackwell.

Schram, W. (1954). How communication works. In W. Schram, *The process and effects of communication* (pp. 3–26). Champaign, IL: University of Illinois Press.

Seiter, J. S., & Weger, H. (2010). The effect of generalized compliments, sex of server, and size of dining party on tipping behavior in restaurants. *Journal of Applied Social Psychology, 40*(1), 1–12.

Self, C. C. (2014). Credibility. In D. W. Stacks, M. B. Salwen (Eds.), *An integrated approach to communication theory and research* (pp. 423–425). London, England: Routeledge.

Shamir, B. (1998). The art of framing: Managing the language of leadership. *The Leadership Quarterly, 9*(1), 123–126.

Shamir, B., House, R. J., & Arthur, M. B. (1993). The motivational effects of charismatic leadership: A self-concept based theory. *Organization Science, 4*(4), 577–594.

Shamir, B., House, R. J., & Arthur, M. B. (1994). The rhetoric of charismatic leadership: A theoritical extension, a case study, and implications for research. *Leadership Quarterly, 5*(1), 25–42.

Shannon, C. E., & Weaver, W. (1949). *The mathematical theory of communication.* Champaign, IL: University of Illinois Press.

Simons, H. W. (1976). *Persuasion; understanding practice and analysis* (1st ed.). Reading, MA: Addison-Wesley.

Simons, H. W. (1986). *Persuasion: Understanding, practice, and analysis* (2nd ed.). New York, NY: Random House.

Simons, H. W., Berkowitz, N. N., & Moyer, J. R. (1970). Similarity, credibility, and attitude change: A review and a theory. *Psychological Bulletin, 73*(1), 1–16.

Swearingen, C. J. (2013). Rhetoric in cross-cultural perspectives. In P. Simnonson, J. Peck, R. T. Craig, & J. P. Jackson (Eds.), *Handbook of communication history* (pp. 115–118). New York, NY: Routeledge.

Taylor, S. E., & Thompson, S. C. (1982). Stalking the elusive "vividness" effect. *Psychological Review, 89*(2), 155–181.

Thistlethwaite, D. L., Haan, H. D., & Kamenetzky, J. (1955). The effects of "directive" and "non-directive" communication procedures on attitudes. *The Journal of Abnormal and Social Psychology, 51*(1), 107–113.

TIME (2012). The top 10 greatest speeches [Online]. Retrieved October 1, 2012 from: http://content.time.com/time/specials/packages/completelist /0,29569,1841228,00.html

Tormala, Z. L., Brinol, P., & Petty, R. E. (2006). When credibility attacks: The reverse impact of source credibility on persuasion. *Journal of Experimental Social Psychology, 42*(5), 684–691.

Willner, A. (1984). *The spellbinders: Charismatic politica leadership*. New Haven, CT: Yale University Press.

Witte, K. (1998). Fear as motivator, fear as inhibitor: Using the extended parallel process model to explain fear appeal successes and failures. In: P. A. Andersen, L. K. Guerrero (Eds.), *The handbook of communication and emotion: Research, theory, applications, and contexts*. San Diego, CA: Academic Press.

Witte, K., & Allen, M. (2000). A meta-analysis of fear appeals: Implications for effective public health campaigns. *Health Education & Behavior, 27*(5), 591–615.

Yadava, J. S. (1987). Communication in India: The tenets of sadharanikaran. In D. L. Kincaid (Ed.), *Communication theory: Eastern and Western perspectives* (pp. 161–171). Albany, NY: Academic Press.

Zimbardo, P. G., Weisenberg, M., Firestone, I., & Levy, B. (1965). Communicator effectiveness in producing public conformity and private attitude change. *Journal of Personality, 33*(2), 233–255.

Contributing Authors

Prof Eleri Jones

Prof Eleri Jones has an academic career spanning more than four decades in fields ranging from nutritional biochemistry to tourism and management. She started teaching in South Glamorgan Institute of Higher Education (SGIHE) in 1984 and was involved in the transition of SGIHE into Cardiff Institute of Higher Education and later, University of Wales Institute, Cardiff; now, Cardiff Metropolitan University. She also served as Director of Research (Associate Dean [Research]) in Cardiff School of Management, has worked with many PhD students worldwide, and has numerous publications to her credit. She is now a Professor Emeritus at the University. Besides this, Prof Jones was the Academic Member on the Welsh Assembly Government's Tourism Advisory Panel advising the Minister of Heritage, a Trustee of Churches Tourism Network Wales and Trade Director for Capital Region Tourism.

Dr Mukul Madahar

Dr Mukul Madahar is currently the MBA Programme Director at the School of Management, Cardiff Metropolitan University. Before joining CMU in February 2003, Mukul worked in industry as a recruitment consultant and on consultancy projects with various organizations. In the past, he was involved with managing the dissertation process as the MBA Dissertation Convener. Mukul has been involved with INFORMS (Institute for Operations Research and Management Sciences), EuSpRIG (European Spreadsheets Risk Interest Group), and AIS (Academy of Information Systems). He is Member of Charted Management Institute (CMI). He is also a Fellow of the HEA (Higher Education Academy) and a member of the Special Interest Group on "Internationalisation".

Index

OTHER TITLES IN OUR CORPORATE COMMUNICATION COLLECTION

Debbie DuFrene, Stephen F. Austin State University, *Editor*

- *Technical Marketing Communication: A Guide to Writing, Design, and Delivery* by Emil B. Towner and Heidi L. Everett
- *Communication for Consultants* by Rita R. Owens
- *Planning and Organizing Business Reports: Written, Oral, and Research-Based* by Dorinda Clippinger
- *Zen and the Art of Business Communication: A Step-by-Step Guide to Improving Your Business Writing Skills* by Susan L. Luck
- *The Essential Guide to Business Communication for Finance Professionals* by Jason L. Snyder and Lisa A.C. Frank
- *Essential Communications Skills for Managers, Volume II: A Practical Guide for Communicating Effectively with All People in All Situations* by Walter St. John and Ben Haskell
- *Producing Written and Oral Business Reports: Formatting, Illustrating, and Presenting* by Dorinda Clippinger
- *How to Write Brilliant Business Blogs, Volume I: The Skills and Techniques You Need* by Suzan St. Maur
- *How to Write Brilliant Business Blogs, Volume II: What to Write About* by Suzan St. Maur

Announcing the Business Expert Press Digital Library

Concise e-books business students need for classroom and research

This book can also be purchased in an e-book collection by your library as

- *a one-time purchase,*
- *that is owned forever,*
- *allows for simultaneous readers,*
- *has no restrictions on printing, and*
- *can be downloaded as PDFs from within the library community.*

Our digital library collections are a great solution to beat the rising cost of textbooks. E-books can be loaded into their course management systems or onto students' e-book readers. The **Business Expert Press** digital libraries are very affordable, with no obligation to buy in future years. For more information, please visit **www.businessexpertpress.com/librarians.** To set up a trial in the United States, please email **sales@businessexpertpress.com**

www.ingramcontent.com/pod-product-compliance
Lightning Source LLC
Chambersburg PA
CBHW071500200326
41519CB00019B/5812